JOB WARS

Confessions
of a
Corporate Recruiter

By
BRIAN NORD

Copyright

Published by Egret Publishing/NFIAssociates and Brian Nord, 15300 W. Howard, PO Box 510422, Berlin, WI 53151.

First published in 2012 by Egret Publishing/NFIAssociates and Brian Nord

Copyright © Brian Nord, 2012. All rights reserved.

Without limiting the rights under copyright reserved above, no part of this publication may be reproduced, stored in or introduced into a retrieval system, or transmitted, in any form or by any means (electronic, mechanical, photocopying, recording, or otherwise), without the prior written permission of both the copyright owner and the above publisher of this book. The scanning, uploading, and distribution of this book via the Internet or via any other means without the permission of the publisher is illegal and punishable by law. Please purchase only authorized electronic editions and do not participate in or encourage electronic piracy of copyrightable materials. Your support of the author's rights is appreciated.

ISBN: 1468181629
ISBN 13: 9781468181623

Library of Congress Control Number: 2012900580
CreateSpace, North Charleston, SC

Table of Contents

Note from the Author	v
Acknowledgements	vii
Introduction	ix
Chapter 1 – Who Does That Nigger Think He Is Anyway?	1
Chapter 2 – Resistance	9
Chapter 3 – The Hammer	15
Chapter 4 – History	23
Chapter 5 – White Side of the Tracks	37
Chapter 6 – Signs	43
Chapter 7 – Shitty	51
Chapter 8 – When Liz Fell	61
Chapter 9 – Dirty Stuff Going On	71
Chapter 10 – Anything Goes	79
Chapter 11 – Going Underground	91
Chapter 12 – Chicken Chasers	103
Chapter 13 – The Wild West	111
Chapter 14 – Got Me	117
Chapter 15 – Student Rights	125
Chapter 16 – Regrets	133
Chapter 17 – Culture	143

Chapter 18 – Companies Lie	157
Chapter 19 – HR Matters?	165
Chapter 20 – Kathy Milton	177
Chapter 21 – Tooth and Nail	187
Chapter 22 – Ambiguous Shades of Gray	197
Chapter 23 – White Guys Too	203
Chapter 24 – Diversity Central	217
Chapter 25 – Solutions	223
Chapter 26 – Stealing Jobs	233
Chapter 27 – The Last Word	247

Note from the Author

I have based this book on my recollections of my life and my experiences in recruiting.

Every aspect of the information I provide about myself and the corporations I worked for is true. The names of companies and people have been changed for the purpose of protecting individuals from retaliation and protecting their privacy. Any similarities to real companies or individuals is purely coincidental.

Should anyone decide to use any of the advice provided, do so with caution and the understanding that there are risks and possible negative consequences.

Citations of specific lawsuits, judgments, investigations, and settlements or related publicized cases of discrimination come from research. In that regard, the names of companies and individuals have already appeared in the public domain in a variety of forums including newspapers, web pages, books, government reporting sites and legal proceedings.

It should be noted that, despite settlements and judgments, many of these companies and individuals never admitted to acts of discrimination or that a culture of discrimination existed. Some of the references cited in the book relate to on-going cases reported in the media, which may or may not have been resolved by the date this book was published.

Acknowledgments

To my best friend and wife of thirty years, Gina, whose love, support, and honesty saved me all those years ago and who continues to provide the inspiration that allows me to move forward. While I am reluctant to use a line from a movie, I must, as it is so utterly perfect to describe the depth of my feelings: "Gina, you make me want to be a better person."

To my son, Dr. Brian Nord Jr., who in his youth, taught me to open my mind.

Introduction

The headline read: "How Employers Weed Out Unemployed Job Applicants, Others, Behind the Scenes."

In an article by reporter Laura Bassett in the January 14, 2011, issue of Internet newspaper the *Huffington Post*, a trial attorney for the federal Equal Employment Opportunity Commission (EEOC) went on record. Bassett wrote; "He said he frequently comes across cases of companies using secret code words in employer profiles that indicate to a staffing firm the race, gender, or age they want in a candidate. "A lot of it's under the radar," the attorney said. "We had a case in Buffalo where a number of former full-time employees at a staffing firm came forward to tell us about how the agency complied with these discriminatory requests; using code words for whites and code words for blacks internally to mask some of it." He also said, "This is what's going on in every state, in every company—the labor laws are ignored. However, catching them is another story. There would have to be wiretaps or someone would have to get inside the company in order to prove what's going on."

It isn't often someone in authority is willing to provide such an emphatic indictment of corporate America as a whole, at least not on the record. Too often, companies that settle with the EEOC are allowed to deny that discrimination took place, despite agreeing to pay thousands or millions of dollars.

After reading this story, I was surprised it didn't go viral. There should have been a firestorm of outrage by the media. There should have been a condemnation from the grass roots. As a corporate recruiter, I expected, at the very least, to come across more job applicants who understood they were playing against a loaded deck and needed to take extraordinary action to have a fair and equal chance at getting a job. However, as evidenced by the way applicants continue to present themselves, making it easy for companies to unfairly weed them out, the majority remain unaware—or unconvinced—that the rules are rigged and they have little alternative but to play the hand they are dealt.

My motivation for this book is to inform the public, just like the journalists who report these trends in the American workplace.

After twenty-two years in corporate recruiting, and being privy to those secret codes and the increasing number of other strategies utilized by hiring managers and companies, I can tell you the employment picture is much worse than what is occasionally revealed in the media. The recruiting, interviewing, and hiring process is inherently corrupt and discriminatory.

Books, websites, and blogs offering job-search advice and strategy are limitless. Some of those hucksterish offerings make claims of job-winning resumes and foolproof answers to interview questions. Others offer specific guides and rules for salespeople, engineers, college grads, executives, middle managers—you name it. They all seem to promise to reveal secrets and inventive strategies that ensure an applicant stands out. However, few, if any, are anything more than the standard job-search guide providing corporate-friendly, generic advice. Whether the information offered actually works for the masses is open for debate.

Job Wars—Confessions of a Corporate Recruiter is not one of those guides. Although the book does contain some advice for job seekers and employees, it is not for the faint of heart, those bent on following the rules, or those who fear breaking them. This book is more of a warning. What you'll find is an unvarnished, often ugly truth about the recruiting and hiring process, which, I guarantee, will be roundly condemned by corporate America because revelation of truth is what it fears the most.

I will also be condemned personally. There is the strong possibility that my career as a corporate recruiter will come to an end. The revelations include everything employers and hiring managers don't want you to know. I expose the corrupt nature of the corporate environment and my role in it, as well as those of other recruiters. I also confess to my own secret codes and strategies, which I utilized to help job applicants beat the unfair system.

You will read about the retaliation I suffered after my attempts to change the system, retaliation that forced me to go underground and work against my employers. More importantly, I offer the philosophy and related strategy of "anything goes." It is a call to arms equal to the anything-goes strategy employers utilize to keep you out and disguise the culture that has little to no interest in contributing to the advancement of equality and fairness.

This book has been in the making since 1996. That's when I returned to corporate America after running my own staffing firm for nine years. My attempts to expose the ugly truth about the recruiting and hiring process have moved in fits and starts since then. Outrage over the depth and breadth of discrimination in the first company I worked for was the motivation for my first attempt at exposure; fear of what it would mean to my future in corporate America forced me to put it in a box. I took it up again after each new employer, job, and outrage. There have been six companies in all, each in a different industry. Over the years, the discriminatory hiring processes never changed and, in some cases, got worse. Today, the basis for unfair treatment and discrimination has expanded to include employment status, personal behavior and lifestyle, medical conditions, education, competence, and political views and affiliations. It's gotten so bad that even white guys, primarily because of age or their own stand against discrimination, are affected.

The last company I worked for was, by far, the worst, maintaining a culture of hatred of women and minorities identical to the era before equal rights laws were enacted. The level of contempt for the law, as well as the level of deceit utilized to cover up, pushed me to finally get this on paper and published.

It's my hope that, at the very least, this book will provide job seekers enough information to take control of their own fate and get that next job—based solely on their qualifications.

Although my thesis includes the belief that corporate leaders don't really care, that they are more interested in quashing any semblance of individualism, there's also a message for company executives, especially those who claim to want an all-inclusive workforce of the best and brightest.

INTRODUCTION

The war being waged against qualified job seekers is also being waged against a growing number of employees who, like me, refuse to go along with the status quo. It forces us to take extraordinary action to beat it or bring it down. The war is also being waged against CEO's.

Hiring managers are the primary perpetrators of this war. Your business, by design or not, is divided into fiefdoms. Void of oversight, when managers make hiring or promotion decisions, they are operating on the basis that their little slice of responsibility within your company is their kingdom. Damn your vision of an all-inclusive workplace of the most qualified. Damn the law and company policy. When no one is watching, as far as they are concerned, they know best, and they make decisions based on what is right for them instead of the business. Their interest is in maintaining their power—regardless of how little they may have.

That paradigm is destroying companies from within. As managers operate on personal fear, bias, hate, and an inflated sense of self-worth, employees who would otherwise give their all become disengaged because of the disheartening reality around them. The proof comes from beyond my own experience and the occasional news story. Consider these statistics:

- According to a Gallup poll, 49 percent of employees are not engaged, and 18 percent are actively disengaged. Source: University of North Carolina, Keenan Flagler Business School, White Paper on Employee Engagement.
- In the summer of 2010, Hewitt reported that nearly 50 percent of the nine hundred

organizations they tracked experienced declines in employee engagement. This was the largest quarterly decline in fifteen years. Source: Conference Board Report

Much of this decline is due to poor leadership. Consider that, according to Towers Watson's 2010 Global Workforce Study (abstracted at www.creativityatwork.com/blog/2010/05/18/mindset-employees-engaged/):

- Only 38 percent of American workers think their leaders have a sincere interest in their well-being.
- Only 47 percent think their leaders are trustworthy.
- Only 4 percent think their leaders inspire and engage them.
- Only 42 percent think senior leaders encourage the development of talent.

Without dramatic intervention, the disengagement and apathy represented by these numbers will only get worse.

CHAPTER 1

Who Does That Nigger Think He is Anyway?

Maybe I should have considered the history of negative reaction when I decided to challenge the status quo out in the open. It was certainly worth considering. The retaliation has included alienation, change of my work conditions, increased monitoring of my work activity, falsification of my performance record, demotion, threats of violence, and termination.

In two instances, termination of my employment was immediate. In one instance, it cost me an annual income of $240,000. The next time around, the loss was a little over $100,000.

The worst of it came after I'd left the company. Unable to make a case for termination based on performance issues, my employers used the pretense of relocation of my position or elimination of my job altogether in order to cover up their retaliation. In order to bolster their defense against my complaint of discrimination, they resorted to trashing my performance report despite promotions and commensurate compensation.

Two employers went as far as adding fake documents to my personnel file. Another employer pulled the standard—accuse the accuser. That company made the claim that I was the one who discriminated against African Americans.

These and other actions threatened to destroy my career and life; they affected my ability to find gainful employment for more than two years. That's how long it took to move my case through the litigation process and catch the company in lies and distortions.

After the last incident, my attorney, John Machulak, Machulak, Robertson & Sodos, S.C. described my willingness to challenge systemic discrimination again as courageous. I disagreed, as none of that negative history entered my mind. Courage comes when one faces danger and uncertainty fully knowing and considering the possibilities.

The first two times I challenged the systemic discrimination, the retaliation and final order of termination were initiated at the very top. With my most recent employer, Uniforms, it began with middle management. The company hierarchy joined the conspiracy only after I'd gone outside the company by filing a discrimination and retaliation complaint with the EEOC.

The regional vice president who led the charge against me did not have the authority to terminate my employment. However, he had the power and influence to affect my job duties and thus my performance. This is how it works: all a manager needs to do is keep a recruiter out of the loop on recruiting needs or give him or her bogus instructions on what positions need to be filled. Essentially, the manager is sending the recruiter on a wild-goose chase and thus forcing him or her to neglect the positions that need to be filled. In some cases, managers simply refuse to interview candidates sent or make the claim a candidate did not meet their needs with the standard statement, "The candidate isn't a fit." After a while, there's a case to be made that the recruiter isn't doing his or her job, as positions remain open and goals are not met. The regional vice president did all of the above and then some, making a case for my termination to those who had the power.

I found out later that employees who'd had the displeasure of working under him in the past had given him the nickname Shitty. It matched how he treated minorities and women. He had pulled some of the same tactics on those employees.

The cause for this attempt to derail my employment occurred on February 23, 2010, during my presentation on recruiting, interviewing, and hiring. I stood in front of a room filled with managers from Shitty's region and called them out for the discrimination they'd perpetrated. The fact that I was the only minority in the room was part of my evidence.

I said, "I can't help but be disappointed as I look around the room and see the lack of diversity. I see the same ratio throughout the company. This does not happen by accident, not in a company with thousands of employees. The company has a policy of equal employment. We all need to do a better job of making it happen."

Then I gave them a few examples of tactics they'd been using. By doing so, I was calling out specific individuals in that room, though I didn't use their names. Every example screamed discrimination, and I made it clear in unmistakable terms that it had to stop.

The reaction was immediate. Within a few seconds of finishing that portion of my presentation, I was given a signal that I only had a few minutes left. I was supposed to have had another thirty. In short, I was pulled from the stage. No one else's time was cut short, either before or after my presentation.

Incidentally, a week earlier, the regional director of human resources, a white male, had conducted the same presentation to another group of managers from the same region. Although he hadn't gone into detail about the lack of diversity the way I did, he'd covered the subject by making the standard lip-service statement approved by the company. He'd been allowed to finish the entire presentation. Like others who'd presented at that meeting and the one I attended, he'd received the customary applause from the audience, as well as a thank you from Shitty.

Applause and a thank you are standard courtesies with little meaning in relation to whether what someone has said is genuinely appreciated. However, those considerations become significant when someone isn't afforded the same courtesy after speaking truth to power. When I left the stage, all was silent.

The extent of the animosity became evident an hour later. As I walked through the hotel lobby, two of the managers from the meeting were huddled in a corner. They abruptly stopped talking when I walked by. But it was too late. I'd already heard one of them say, "Who does that nigger think he is anyway?" The other was still nodding his head when I stopped and glared at them. I should have been upset, but I wasn't. The nigger comment wasn't a surprise. Based on everything I had experienced over the past eighteen months, I'd known it was only a matter of time before it surfaced.

At this company, some managers used code words, double standards, pretext, and other covert activity to feed their discriminatory bias. Others openly showed their dislike for minorities and contempt for women. Countless scenarios played out at various levels of the organization.

A district sales manager in Florida confirmed to me that the lack of minority salespeople was intentional. The culture-think included the belief that white business people would not purchase goods from minorities, and he specifically referred to African Americans. He also noted that some of the Hispanic route drivers hired ended up in predominantly Hispanic areas. A general manager in Georgia instructed me to stop sending "old guys." He warned that if I repeated what he said, he would just deny it and we would be "done."

The North region demonstrated the worst of it after Shitty was promoted to vice president in 2009. When I attended a meeting in April of that year, some of us gathered for drinks in the hotel bar the first night. As I approached their table, five general managers couldn't control their laughter as one of them said to me, "Over the phone, you sound like a white guy with a stick stuck up his ass." The comment was in response to another GM, Carl, telling me how surprised he was that I was black. While the others laughed, he apologized. He was concerned he may have said something offensive about blacks during one of our previous conversations when he thought I was "a stuck-up white guy."

Even then, I knew what was later confirmed by the reaction during the meeting and the nigger comment: minorities were viewed in a certain stereotype, and when it came to African Americans, they were only tolerated if they stayed in their place. In the company's eyes, I'd crossed the line with my presentation. The affect it would have on my future there would materialize in the weeks and months to come.

None of it mattered to me by then. That presentation was just the latest of actions I'd taken against the worst culture of discrimination I had ever experienced. Nine months earlier, I had lifted a self-imposed restraint on coaching job applicants so that they could beat the unfair system. Management's reaction at that fateful meeting and thereafter only strengthened my resolve to continue that practice until I left the company.

If Machulak's definition of courage can be applied, it would be a more appropriate description for my actions after he'd confirmed that I may have been retaliated against. In addition to filing the EEOC complaint, I decided to stay on the job until it was resolved.

Many people simply walk away from the job when they are confronted with discrimination or after they file a complaint, and I don't blame them. The environment gets nasty very quickly. Friends and allies disown you as soon as the word gets out. In this case, considering what I'd experienced for simply calling corporate management out, I could assume that all hell was going to break loose once they learned I'd filed a complaint.

The irony here is that I had already planned on leaving the company without making a fuss. If the retaliation hadn't taken place, and if my boss, Liz, who was also my friend, hadn't refused to take the proper action to deal with it, I would have followed through, primarily out of respect for the ten-year relationship.

I'd informed Liz a few weeks prior to the February meeting that it wouldn't be more than three or four months before I called it quits. The issue came up as a result of a larger conversation about all the chaos and lack of continuity in the organization, hallmarks of just about everything we did. The lack of uniformity regarding how job applicants were selected was a contributing factor to the lack of diversity in the company. Managers took cunning advantage of the chaos. One of their favorite tactics was to change interview procedures and increase or change the qualification requirements when a minority, female, or older candidate was presented.

The last comment I'd made to Liz during what had turned into a heated argument was, "I'm tired of walking into meetings and being the only minority."

I stayed to fight because of the aforementioned history. I confess that I also stayed to make up for those times in the past when I hadn't fought.

The existence of a company culture in 2010 that was worse than what I'd encountered in 1996 when I came back to corporate America, could be blamed, in part, on the fact that people like me had walked away. I promised myself to follow in the footsteps of one of the complainants who'd won a historic discrimination case against Texaco back in the mid-nineties. When a reporter had asked him if he would be leaving the company after the settlement was reached, as others had, he'd said, "No, I'm going to stay. Someone has to keep an eye on them to make sure they live up to what they promised."

Uniforms promised an inclusive workforce. They promised zero tolerance for discrimination. They promised protection for anyone who spoke up and challenged. I was going to do my best to make them live up to it.

CHAPTER 2

Resistance

"*I became convinced that non-cooperation with evil is as much a moral obligation as is cooperation with good.*" Martin Luther King Jr.

The president of the nonprofit company I worked for in 1981 said this in his monthly newsletter: "Despite his young age, Brian comes by his retail experience honestly."

He gave a rundown of my experience in conjunction with my age because it was hard for him to fathom how someone so young could have the kind of insight and vision to achieve, as he put it, "the miraculous transformation in the appearance of the main store and the resulting improvement of revenue and employee attitudes." He was referring to the infectious pride and motivation that seemed to consume employees.

The key phrase—"comes by his retail experience honestly"—also describes how I come by my rebellious, righteous indignation and justification for fighting the evil of workplace discrimination. I come by that honestly, as well.

It would probably be more grandiose to say that it was the sentiment of that quote from Martin Luther King Jr. alone that inspired my standing up against the power of a corrupt system. Although those words, along with everything else Dr. King and people like him believed in, have helped form the basis for my conscience, more of the credit goes to my mother.

Before you get the wrong idea, I have to tell you this isn't one of those "my mother is the rock who supported me and gave me the courage to stand and be counted" kind of situation. Neither is it a case of "mommy dearest" or condemnation of an abusive childhood that destroyed my spirit. To the contrary, despite our differences and some god-awful moments that would be described as abusive by today's standards, any psychological scars, which may have resulted, are mitigated by other, positive effects. To be certain, it was not a nurturing environment. However, I can attribute my survival of that abuse as a contributing factor to my resolve and resilience in dealing with the hardships I would face later in life.

My mother and I have been at odds for as long as I can remember. Beyond the aforementioned, mostly, it is because I have considered myself equal enough to stand up to any injustice I encountered. She doesn't believe that equality and the rights that come with it matter. Our last falling out was in late 1999, and we haven't spoken a civil word since, but that's another story.

RESISTANCE

Suffice it to say that, based on the way I was brought up and the related punishment and ridicule I received, my mother doesn't approve of stands I have taken since, or the way I have taken them. Because of that, she wouldn't approve of me giving her credit either. However, whether she likes it or not, she deserves the credit, because I did as she did instead of as she said. She gets credit for my automatic reaction to evil, as well as my resistance to the idea that black people, in particular, are only acceptable if they act in a way that is accepted by rules of a white society, which are often unfair and demeaning.

I was seven when President Kennedy was assassinated. I remember it like it was yesterday because Mom was in tears for days before, during, and after watching the funeral on TV. I also remember it because it was the day I learned for the first time that white people didn't like "colored" people. I learned, as well, that there was a certain way black people were supposed to conduct themselves in order to have the chance of being accepted by white people or considered different from those other black people.

At some point during the funeral, there was a knock on the back door. It was Kevin, a kid from the neighborhood. He wanted to know if we could come out to play. My mother swung the door open. I can still picture her with her hands on her hips, holding that tissue, with the red nose and besotted eyes. Angrily, she told Kevin, "This isn't a day for playing. The president died. We're watching his funeral. That's what you should be doing. Go home!" Then she slammed the door in his face.

As she ushered me and my three brothers back into the living room, she said, "That's why white people can't stand colored people; they don't respect nothin'."

The implication was that all black people were like Kevin. There was something wrong with them, and therefore it was justifiable for white people to consider them less than equal. If that were true, didn't it also mean that there was something wrong with my family—at least, my dad, my brothers, and I? Our skin was brown, just like Kevin's. Did it mean that Mom felt the same way about us, yet considered herself different and better because she was only half-black and had inherited the skin of her white father?

You might imagine that I didn't consider these questions or reach any conclusions at the time—I was only seven. That incident and others like it stayed with me and festered for years as I came of age and gained experience that allowed me to form my own view of the world. As I look back, I wonder if the beatings, demeaning labels, and insults were as much a reflection of the animosity she felt toward blacks as they were an attempt to beat the rebellion out of me.

It would explain why I wasn't given the chance to provide an explanation for my actions before the hand came across my cheek, knocking me to the floor, when I was in the second grade. One of the nuns at the catholic school we attended reported that I had kicked another nun in the shin. Sister McCalla had watched from a second-floor window as I'd crossed the street in the middle of the block during recess. When the crossing guard had tried to give me a detention slip for breaking the rules, I'd denied it had been me. Sister McCalla intervened. She was flabbergasted by my denial, which continued even after she said she saw me. She called me a "little black liar." I called her a liar back. She slapped me almost as hard as my mother did hours later. I kicked her and ran off.

OK, I did lie. Did that give her the right to physically harm me? Did she have the right to call me a "black liar" as opposed to just liar? I wasn't taking that. And neither were my parents. Mom insisted they never lay a hand on one of her children again; corporal discipline was the sole providence of my parents. During the drive home, Mom gave me the silent treatment (which often lasted for days in that kind of situation). The moment we got home, I was on the floor holding my face. That weekend, the belt came out. My father had the unenviable duty of doling out punishment days after something happened, a job he accepted reluctantly. As often as Mom lashed out at the moment, she would also say, "Wait until your father comes home." Because of his two jobs—one of them a second shift—we only had Dad's company on the weekend. And, for many years, until around age thirteen, the weekend often began with that leather belt coming down on one of us.

My understanding of how Mom may have categorized colored people by their actions in relation to the acceptance of white society came years later, after Martin Luther King Jr. was assassinated. I was too afraid to approach her at the time, but I wanted to ask why there were no tears for Reverend King. The other question I wanted to ask was why did I have no idea King existed until my oldest brother Bob, five years my senior, came running down the stairs to announce that King's assassination had just been reported on the radio?

It wasn't until the summer before I entered high school when I finally broached the subject. By then, I had gotten into a few scrapes at school. Not physical fights, but battles of wills with the school administration over student rights issues.

My mother's view on Martin Luther King Jr. was not untypical at the time. I read somewhere that there were just as many black people who didn't like King as those who revered him. Some thought he was dangerous. Mom responded to my questions by saying she thought he was a troublemaker who made it harder for black people. It was an astounding statement considering Mom could have been described the same way—and probably was by some—because she was a hero of the housing civil rights movement of the sixties. She'd faced down the status quo just as King had. Her personal battle line was that which separated suburban Milwaukee from the city, the same line that separated whites from blacks. It had been the one and only time she'd refused to keep her head down and go along the way a "good black" was expected to. Her actions had defied everything she'd taught us about how blacks were supposed to act in order to be acceptable to white society.

CHAPTER 3

The Hammer

I confess that my extreme liberalism is an Achilles heel when it comes to forging allies and friendships within the workplace. My automatic inclination to assume the best in people and take them at face value until their actions prove otherwise is a product of my youth, born as an act of defiance to some of those lessons my parents tried to teach me.

My parents are cautiously optimistic, if not pessimistic, when they are confronted with new faces. An automatic protective shield comes up, just in case the new face turns out to have the same character as the last evil person who crossed their path. They assume that the new face, smiling or not, is nothing but a mask to cover the ill intent beneath. They are more inclined to maintain this view until the individual or group proves otherwise. I defied that perspective because it often had a discriminatory component, which also made for some confusion as messages from my mother, especially, were contradictory: don't act like the kind of black that will be disliked by white people, yet be cautious of white people even if you "act right."

Also, I confess that I have an inflated view of my ability to judge character and thereby choose carefully those whom I call friends. I have been known to brag of a thoughtful deliberation process as the reason I am able to make the right judgment, overlook, even forgive, negatives in an individual in favor of what I identify as the core of his or her character. The reality is I am wrong far more often than I am right. Because of the damage inflicted by those who turned out to be different than they pretended to be, I have to admit the possibility that my parents and the large number of people like them are closer to being on the right track than I am. I have the propensity to hold onto whatever positive view I have of someone, often even after they have engaged in actions that proved otherwise.

This information is important when it comes to understanding why I befriended Liz, my former boss, and others like her. At the very least, her actions were such that I should have moved the trust needle to neutral until the whole of her character came to light. There were moments like this incident with a fellow employee at Kprints, Kim, that should have raised the caution flag.

As a human resource generalist, Kim knew the field backward and forward. When it came to doing her job, she was the consummate professional, and that was the only side our boss, Liz, knew. These facts allowed me to not pass judgment on Kim's personal life or the fact that she enjoyed sharing it with just about everyone.

Liz didn't know that Kim, by her own admission, was an alcoholic, or that she was a sex addict. Liz didn't know that Kim's sexual exploits and need for physical punishment and manipulation by her lover, whom she described as "her master," were well-known throughout the rank and file at Kprints in the Chicago market.

Even newcomer human resource generalist Sherri got a taste of Kim's personal life within days of joining the company. In Sherri's office, Kim declared her love for the regional vice president of sales, Parker, whom she'd seduced, she disclosed. Kim even provided details of the consummation of their relationship, including the way she'd straddled the leather chair in his regional office one night. She told that story through tears of self-pity. Parker was not into the 'master' role or any of the pain-inflicting acts Kim had begged him to perform. He'd declared her a freak to her face, ending any possibility they would ever be a couple.

Not long after, Kim's distress over the break-up was part of the reason she'd had a few too many during a flight from Tennessee to Chicago. A flight attendant, concerned for her safety, insisted she could not leave in her current state. Kim agreed to call a friend to pick her up. However, instead of calling a friend named Liz, she pushed the speed dial on her cell that connected to her boss named Liz. She must have rambled for several minutes before Liz explained whom she was talking to.

I happened to be attending a meeting with Liz in Boston when the call came. She was visibly irritated when she explained the circumstances. Liz believed Kim's conduct was a violation of company policy. There was a line in the manual that held employees accountable for behavior off the job if it had the potential to reflect badly on the company. Sex in the office with an executive was certainly grounds for termination, but Liz was not in the loop on any of that part of Kim's behavior. When Liz solicited my opinion about the plane incident, I argued that being drunk on a plane on her own time, unidentifiable as a Kprints employee, was not the company's business.

This is just one example of the hard-ass persona that earned Liz the nickname The Hammer. Others referred to Liz as "the bitch in the ivory tower." They believed she was unreasonable when she held steadfastly to the letter of company policy. The Hammer was a more apt description in that there was not a chauvinistic connotation to the term. It described the relentless way in which she confronted wrongdoing in her capacity as regional human resource manager.

There's no question Liz was rough in her delivery. When someone tried to excuse their way out of unacceptable behavior or flat-out lied about the circumstances, she was fond of using the phrase "if it looks like a duck and sounds like a duck, it's a duck." Liz was one of those people who needed to be certain that the person under scrutiny knew that not only what he or she did was wrong, but also that nobody was fooled by his or her denial. Equally, Liz was all business in the right way. She didn't believe that employees needed to be cheerleaders, as if working for the company was the center of their lives, or to socialize for the purpose of providing that façade of commitment to job and company. She was scornful of those who drank during company gatherings or social events. Do the job, work hard—these were her tenets of a good employee.

Others who held a less favorable view of Liz pointed to the times when her strict adherence to the rules skewed her judgment. I sympathized with some of that reasoning, however I defended her adherence to rules claiming it was an admirable quality necessary to ensure accountability. The lack of accountability is growing like a plague and contributes to the conditions within corporate America that allow discrimination to exist. I also argued that they missed the fact that she was aware of the possibility that she might be wrong and, therefore, sought advice from others, like me. That's what she was doing in the Kim situation. Although she allowed that one incident at the airport to cloud her overall perception of Kim, totally discounting the professionalism Kim otherwise demonstrated, she listened to my dissenting view and took no action. She made similar adjustments to her decision-making throughout the time we worked together.

I first met Liz in October of 2000. She had been promoted to human resource manager and transferred in from Michigan to the regional office in Chicago. I had just been promoted to regional management recruiter. Within a few months, a reorganization made her my immediate supervisor. I soon became her confidant, and she mine, on business and personal issues. We saw eye to eye on the virtues and failings of the corporate environment, and we did our best to influence it positively within our areas of responsibility. The friendship was such that it survived my promotion to corporate and her voluntary separation from the company a few years later and relocation to Georgia from the Midwest.

During the Kprints days, she was one of the reasons I survived for as long as I did. Even though I had to be careful about how much I reported about the discrimination I witnessed, she was one of two people in authority I could say anything to at all. When I did, she handled the situation in a way that didn't involve me. That ensured my ability to work with managers without being labeled a snitch or someone who could not be trusted.

To be certain, Liz had her quirks, and some of the negative opinions about her were justified. She did fly off the handle occasionally, and she did rely too much on the letter of the employee manual. However, I chose to overlook those flaws, just as I would hope people would overlook similar flaws I might have after considering the whole of my character.

To be fair to those naysayers who thought the worst of her, I have to confess that my opinion may be skewed. It was Liz who recognized early on my superior recruiting experience and made it possible for me to avoid a reorganization and downsizing. It was one of the few times she went against the letter of company policy. Last one hired, first one fired was the rule. That meant I would have been the first to go. But, as she told me at the time, "I'm really glad I was able to keep you. I have always believed that experience and performance trump time on the job."

A year later, when she went on maternity leave, I was the one she recommended as her temporary replacement as regional hr. manager. That same year, she nominated me for human resource employee of the year. The award included a $15,000 one-time bonus on top of my regular bonus and annual salary increase.

THE HAMMER

I went to work for Liz at Uniforms based on the positives in her character demonstrated during those Kprints days. I held on to my early determination of her character, choosing to totally forget the negatives. It was a choice that eventually proved to be one of my worst ever.

CHAPTER 4

History

From company to company, the circumstances and conditions I worked under have varied over the years. However, what happened at Uniforms has been the story of my work life.

I went to work for Liz at Uniforms to escape the retaliation I was experiencing at the Restaurant Group, a multi-brand restaurant-operating company with more than one thousand locations nationwide, where I held the position of director of recruiting. The retaliation there began for the same reason it would later start at Uniforms.

In November of 2007, my friend Meg was in attendance at a meeting at the Restaurant Group when I confronted the systemic discrimination there the same way

I would at Uniforms; as part of a presentation on recruiting and hiring to more than three hundred managers and executives, including the CEO.

I'd hired Meg as a management recruiter a few months earlier. She was a witness to the type of incidents I described at the meeting. These included:

- An e-mail written by one of the general managers complaining about the number of minority job applicants he had to interview, demonstrating the culture of disdain for African Americans.
- An e-mail sent by a district manager to one of my recruiters rejecting an applicant because of age. In the email the manager stated, "this guy is so old he owes Moses a nickel."
- A disturbing double standard. In Dallas, Texas, a drug conviction revealed during a background check of a white job applicant didn't have any effect on his hiring, but in Richmond, Virginia, a minority candidate with the same type of conviction was eliminated from consideration. This showed that there were exceptions made for white males, even when it came to criminal behavior. The common opinion was that anyone involved in drugs might also be desperate for money to maintain the habit. That made him or her a high risk for theft of restaurant proceeds. However, without exception, when the applicant was a minority, the standard was strictly upheld.
- Discrimination so pervasive that, even in highly populated Hispanic areas of southern Texas, there were remarkably few Hispanics elevated beyond assistant manager.

- Additional discrimination. Discrimination against minorities, women, and because of age was just part of the problem. It was company policy to disqualify job applicants based on criminal records and credit history, without following the legal criteria of whether the crimes and circumstances pertained to the jobs they would be performing. This had the potential to affect everyone, regardless of whether someone was part of a protected class.

In the meeting, I referenced those and other open acts of discrimination, as well as the disparity in the hiring process. I offered my observations and suggestions for a remedy in as diplomatic terms as possible. The buzz phrase used by many who advocated diversity and inclusion was "the business case." It was advantageous for a business to have diversity, especially if that business relied on a diverse customer base.

One of the examples I offered to make this point was competitor Darden Restaurant Corporation. They were highly successful, even during what we would find out in the following years was a difficult economic time. Part of that success could be attributed to their broad diversity, including the board of directors. Darden's commitment to diversity went back to its founder in the 1930s. Even during that period in American history, when it was legal to discriminate against blacks, he hired anyone who was willing to work, including blacks.

With Darden as a comparison, I noted that the lack of diversity within Restaurant Group was bad for business. The reasons for the discrimination put the company at risk for lawsuits, not to mention a greater loss of business.

Admittedly, no one solicited my detailed observations at Restaurant Group any more than they would two years later at Uniforms. In fact, in a roundabout way, permission was taken away.

The original PowerPoint slides I'd submitted for approval had included specific bullet points on the issue, including details of the company's acts of discrimination and disparity in the hiring process. All references to diversity beyond the single bullet point had been eliminated when I got the approved version back.

Aside from allowing me to finish my entire presentation, the reaction from the Restaurant Group management to what I had to say would mirror that of the folks at Uniforms. No standard applause, no thank you from the CEO before he introduced the next presenter, and no discussion.

Unlike Uniforms, there was no pretense about wanting diversity and inclusion. Sure, they had the same policies of equal opportunity, and we advertised it on our job postings and company brochures just like everyone else. However, no one acknowledged what was obvious from the racial makeup of that room. The silence from the CEO and other executives, combined with several whispered comments of amazement and approval from a few other lower-ranking employees who had been with the company a number of years, told me I was in trouble. A vendor from PepsiCo, who happened to be African American, pulled me to the side after the meeting and actually shook my hand. "That took guts. No one has ever talked to them like that," he said. "You know you have to watch your back, right?" Dave, a general manager in training whom I'd recruited a month earlier, warned me, as well. He'd sat at the table next to the

CEO, Clint. He'd overheard conversation that had included complaints about my comments and somebody at the table saying, "This guy's gotta go!"

A week later, I received the e-mail from the CEO. "Due to the importance of the director position, we need to have it based at our corporate office in Dallas. If you are unable to make that commitment, your employment will end on January 7, 2008." In addition, I would have to make the move at my own expense.

He knew I couldn't make that commitment. Everybody knew it. Living in Milwaukee, Wisconsin, was a condition of my employment agreed upon when I'd taken the job a year earlier. It had been reaffirmed not more than ten days prior to my presentation, when I'd received a $10,000 pay increase, a vote of confidence in my performance, as well as an enticement to make sure I stayed with the company. Other managers were bailing with each new sign of additional financial trouble for the company.

This is what gets me more than anything else. Before I came to the Restaurant Group—in fact, the reason I was brought into the company—was because their recruiting was in total disarray. Management turnover resulted in over one hundred forty of their thousand restaurant management positions left open every month. The recruiting strategies I instituted reduced that number to an average of thirteen by the time the meeting in which I outlined the company's discriminatory practices took place.

After an executive staff meeting in May of that first year, the senior vice president of human resources called to tell me how excited everyone was, that one unit president had even said, "I haven't even met this guy, but I'll tell you right now, he's a superstar. We can't keep up with the candidate flow. And the quality is better than anything we've seen." I saved the company tens of thousands on recruiting expenses, and the increasing stability of the management workforce saved them tens of thousands in training and development costs. The reason it gets me is I have always been under the delusion that money trumps everything— including a black guy stepping over their imaginary line, calling out discrimination. If I ever felt safe about challenging the status quo, it was because of that delusion.

Meg had responded with a slightly patronizing laugh the first time I'd offered that view. She's the one who'd first used the word "delusional" when I'd made the same argument to her years earlier to describe my amazement at how quickly FSfoods had ended my employment in 1996 in a similar manner. By FSfoods own description, I had saved them hundreds of thousands of dollars with efficiencies I'd brought to their recruiting process. I was certain money far out weighed any negatives they perceived about my race and again, that I was safe because of it.

"Think about it," she'd said. "If you looked like one of them, no problem, you might be safe talking about discrimination and the fact that you made them bucket loads of money would have put you on the untouchable list. But a black guy telling a room full of white people who begrudge you being there in the first place? C'mon! Their racism trumps anything good you bring to the table including saving them big money!"

We became friends during our Kprints days, and she was one of the few I asked to critique this book each time I took up writing it. If what happened at Uniforms was a déjà vu of what had occurred at Restaurant Group, then what happened at Restaurant Group was a déjà vu of my problems at FSfoods fourteen years earlier.

I referred to the FSfoods ordeal on a number of occasions as the primary reason I had promised myself that I wasn't going to lead the charge if I ever encountered discrimination like that again. Contradictorily, I also cited that situation as the reason I thought nothing would come of simply talking about the need for diversity in some of the processes and systems in place, as I would at every company going forward.

FSfoods didn't have a problem with pointing out discrimination or having in-depth conversation about it. Dialogue about the culture, specific incidents, the effects on the business, and how to fix things were endless.

I saw and heard everything as the national recruiting manager there. Can't hire women because the job is just too rough for them, they should be barefoot and pregnant. Can't hire blacks because they don't have black people to sell to. They considered hiring Hispanics if they didn't look Hispanic and did not have an accent.

Twelve months into the job I was dealing with it on their terms, until the call came. The division manager on the other end of the line obviously hadn't received the memo (maybe because none had gone out), since he thought nothing of telling me to stop sending him black people to interview. "In the past, I've tried hiring blacks in the warehouse," he said. "They're all lazy. So stop sending them, because I won't hire any."

After finishing that call, I dialed my boss, field HR manager Todd, and unloaded. That was when I threatened to do what they considered the unthinkable. "It has to stop," I said. "I'm not going to continue to listen to people denigrate African Americans. It's been eleven months! The company keeps promising to do something about this and, yet, here we are." Then I said, "You know, I could have easily gone to the EEOC with all kinds of evidence. I haven't because I believed you when you said things were going to change."

In between those two jobs (Restaurant Group and FSfoods), I worked at Kprints. Meg read how, at the time I was planning to make the move to Restaurant Group from Kprints, the newly appointed vice president of field human resources did solicit details, and not just from me. When she asked the question, there were six field human resource directors on the weekly conference call. It took place more than a week after she and I had participated in what would be the last of the panel interviews at the corporate office.

The panel had been set up to give executive staff a say in hires and promotions for district management positions. I didn't know if she was aware of it, but the primary reason for the panel process was to try to make some headway in the expansion of diversity within the ranks of upper management.

Sean, the vice president of field human resources at the time, sold the idea to corporate executives based on my concern that a number of qualified job applicants for district manager positions were rejected when I sent them to interview with individual VPs. Most of the time, it was a woman or a minority. If a reason for the rejection was provided, it defied logic or standards and was often contradictory to decisions they had made to hire others.

There was one instance where a female candidate was rejected because her multi-unit experience was with Wendy's restaurants. Yet, the same VP hired another candidate who'd come from Wendy's. The candidate had less experience and was a white male.

Although some of those regional vice presidents would be involved in the panel interviews, so would their boss, Ander. Sean's deal was, "Let them try to get away with that kind of stuff in front of him, he'll cut them to shreds. You bring the right candidates, they'll get hired." Sean was right, at least during those sessions when Ander was in the room.

To be certain, I stacked the deck with women and minorities. Every one of them was more than qualified, meeting the top-grade standard expected. There were three of those panel interviews over eleven months; during that period, more women and minorities were hired than at any time before or since.

True to Sean's observation, VPs notorious for making poor decisions were held in check by Ander's presence. However, when he left the room, it was a different story. During one session, as quickly as the door closed behind him, what I called "the boardroom massacre" began.

Job candidate Robert was disqualified because of his age. The pretense used by the regional vice president who refused to consider him was a single incident in the Robert's history. Three jobs and thirteen years earlier, he had followed his boss to a position at Blockbuster. The job only lasted six months. Since that time, he had worked two other regional-level positions and stayed at each company for six and seven years respectively. But, according to the VP, he would jump from Kprints as soon as that boss who poached him all those years ago came calling.

Barb, another applicant, made the mistake of mentioning that she had grandchildren. Even Sean was dismayed at how quickly the interview came to an end. The questions just stopped coming. They would eventually say she "wasn't a fit." No other reason was given.

Candidate Karen indicated she was gay when she mentioned her domestic partner. The corporate brass would collectively decide she wasn't a fit because she'd used the word "bullshit" during one of her answers. The exact word was one of the many staple profanities used throughout the company by males all the time.

This was the kind of idiotic reasoning the new VP saw after she took over for Sean. She was noticeably pissed because one of the candidates recommended by the panel had been rejected by the regional vice president in favor of someone who wasn't anywhere near as qualified and, in fact, had some serious flaws in his job performance. Both candidates had been internal. The candidate rejected was Hispanic, and his performance had been picture-perfect for promotion. "What's going on here?" the new VP asked us during a weekly conference call. "What good does it do to have the candidates interview with the executive team and not get hired? I'm concerned because the candidate recommended is Hispanic."

She didn't note that the one hired was a white male, but I knew. I'd processed the offer. After a few moments of silence, she said, "Well, I want you to think about it. If anyone can give me some understanding of how I should look at this, I'd like to hear from you."

After the call, I sent her an e-mail that laid it out for her. The vice president in question was the one who made it clear: minorities couldn't do the district manager job. He felt the same way about women. I didn't leave it there. I gave her other examples of bogus decisions by hiring managers at various levels. I provided a history of the type of discrimination I had witnessed by field managers, which had been the catalyst for the establishment of the panel interview process in the first place.

Maybe I'd been fooled by the open forum in which she'd asked the question. She'd broached the subject during a conference call with the entire field of HR directors. From that, I assumed she was one of the "good guys" and I could, therefore, be totally honest. But maybe my observations and attitude about the failure of field managers to adhere to the CEO's strong message about diversity was more information than she'd wanted. Maybe I shouldn't have gone as far as to name names. For all I knew, some of those people had been hand-picked by executives she didn't want to tangle with. Maybe they were close associates of hers. Whatever the case, there seemed to be a change in communication with her after that, and the subject was never broached again. The only retaliation I can point to is the fact that talk of my promotion, which had been ongoing, came to an end.

Meg would say it was the knowledge of this history that had her convinced there would never be a time when I wouldn't directly confront a discriminatory culture. That's why she cut me off when I tried to apologize for speaking up at Restaurant Group. The apology was due to the fact that the retaliation that would eventually end my employment also affected her, as it did anyone who'd been associated with me.

Meg used my own words to explain why she knew the same scenario would play out no matter what else I did to thwart the daily acts of discrimination. She knew it, and she considered that knowledge when she decided to take the job. She considered the risk of being associated with me, if anything came to pass.

Meg pointed to one of the first things I'd written in early drafts of my book to explain my reasons for challenging the system despite the risk: "I have seen and experienced enough to know that discrimination and the way it plays out in corporate America is a terrible scourge gnawing at the moral soul of our society. In some cases, it's unrecognized. In others, companies simply refuse to acknowledge it. Either way, allowing it to exist threatens the future of women and minorities. All of us have the moral responsibility to speak up and challenge the status quo. To do otherwise would be criminal."

Meg, of course, was right in all of this. And because of my African American heritage, I believe that I have a personal stake in this issue, as well.

A few years back I took an assessment test which was designed to determine an individual's racial preference. Here are the results.

"You have completed the African American /European American IAT.

Your Result: *Your data suggest little to no automatic preference between Black and White people.*

Thank you for your participation. Just below is a breakdown of the scores generated by others. Most respondents find it easier to associate African American with "Bad" and European American with "Good"."

The first point of interest is the result, which suggests I have little to no automatic preference between black and white people. The other point of interest is the overall statistics, that came with the report. They indicate that 70 percent of respondents had some level of automatic preference for white people over black people. Of that number, 27 percent had a strong preference. Another 27 percent had a moderate preference, while 17 percent had a slight preference. Only 12 percent had any kind of preference for black people compared to white people. My "little to no preference" fell in the seventeenth percentile.

I took the IAT (Implicit Association Test) out of curiosity after watching a CNN series on race in America. My point is this: despite my lack of preference, I cannot disregard the fact that as an African American, I am affected by society's negative view of African Americans, and I am compelled to do something about it. Especially when I take into consideration my belief that conditions for some minorities—like African Americans and Hispanics, who have lingered on the edge of economic calamity as victims of the disparity—are at a crossroads where they are at real risk of becoming a permanent underclass. If we look at the current state of the job market and the related deterioration of the middle class, many would argue they already have.

CHAPTER 5

White Side of the Tracks

The terms "redlining" and "steering"—used to describe the practice of keeping minorities from purchasing real estate in white neighborhoods and limiting, if not denying, access of financial services to minorities—didn't exist in the mid-1960s. They wouldn't come into regular use until the end of the decade. My mother became a civil rights hero of sorts as one of the early challengers to the status quo. She was the first to fight for the right to purchase property and build in the middle of an all-white neighborhood in suburban Milwaukee.

Mom was born Betty Farris outside of wedlock to a poor black woman who'd had a brief encounter with a white man. He'd left town after hearing of the pregnancy. Mom's mother died from complications during childbirth. Mom spent the better part of her youth as an outcast because of the skin color she'd inherited from her father.

What many considered a curse back in those days became an advantage when she entered the workforce after bearing four children in the 1950s. She passed for white when it suited her. Despite an education that had ended with high school, she spoke well, and she was classically beautiful. Appearance alone allowed her passage to the white side of the tracks, the northern suburbs where my parents expected to build a home and advance their upward movement in American society.

Dad was one of nine children born to a life of severe poverty as sharecroppers on a farm in Birmingham, Alabama. After an eighth-grade education—Dad could barely read and write at age sixteen—he decided to strike out on his own to relieve the family burden of too many mouths to feed. He was twenty-two by the time he made his way to Ohio, where he met Mom.

By the time I knew him, whatever charm he must have possessed in order to woo her was long gone. I'm certain this was because of the onus of the life dictated by his dark skin.

My dad is a great man. Despite the odds, he found a path to ensure that his family had it better than he did—much better. There's a song - I forget who sings it – with a line that goes like this: *"My papa is a great old man, I can see him with a shovel in his hand – education he never had, he did wonders when the times got bad"*. It's a tribute to hard work, perseverance, and strength of character, and it's how I have always viewed – "my old man".

He worked second shift, so when my parents decided to build a home, the task of viewing lots was left to my mother. She would go during the week, after a day's work at her office job with the county welfare department. Land was plentiful, and she was urged at every opportunity by the real estate agent to make a commitment. Of course, she couldn't make any decision without Dad, so she scheduled an appointment for the weekend when they could review the lot selections together. As soon as those real estate agents saw my father, the lots suddenly became unavailable.

When they were finally able to make it over that part of the hurdle and secure a lot with a down payment, lending institutions refused services. Intervention by civil rights groups eventually resulted in a partnership with a local savings and loan.

By the time Martin Luther King Jr.'s assassination hit the newswires, the Nord family had endured resistance not uncommon during those days. Before and after we moved into our new home, there were death threats. We were threatened with bombs. A slug from a twenty-two caliber rifle lodged in the frame of the picture window on the main floor. Other acts of vandalism included cars pulling into the lot, circling the dirt yard, and then screaming off, throwing up clouds of dust and rock that peppered the front of the house. On three occasions we woke the next morning to find piles of garbage in the front yard.

Some believed it was mom's celebrity that caused the negative attention. She'd appeared on the local TV station, giving a guest editorial on our ordeal. However, my best recollection is that the disturbances caused by those few true haters actually ignited an outpouring of support from neighbors at the end of that first summer.

One late morning in August, my father, despite having worked a double shift, skipped sleep and began laying sod that had been delivered for our front and back yards. With just two days before he needed to return to work, he knew that covering that half-acre with a work crew comprised of Mom and four kids would be a stretch. But he was determined to get it all done, evidenced by his feverish pace, despite the heat of the August sun.

I remember whining, along with two of my siblings, over the difficulty of the task. I also remember my numerous trips to the comfort of the house to quench my thirst. Dad was in the middle of questioning my constant need for that much water when he was interrupted by two cars pulling up. Men, women, and children poured out. Little was said. They just jumped in and began to lend a hand.

It wasn't long before other neighbors arrived, often without saying a word, just reaching for some sod and eventually taking over the task from us four kids. Some of the people were familiar to my parents, but most weren't. What had been a chore that would have had us working well into Sunday night was completed within a few hours. It left the rest of the day for kids to play and neighbors to enjoy the barbecue and other food that had accompanied many who'd showed up that day.

According to my oldest brother, it was the work of the likes of Martin Luther King Jr. that had won us the ability to live the middle-class life in that neighborhood at that time. Mom's view was that we had made it in spite of King.

I was twelve then. The Nord family was living the American dream. My parents taught us to play by the rules, as they did. Our life on Calumet Road was testament to that regime. Even earlier, we'd lived in a racially diverse neighborhood, although it had been mostly white. I had few black friends, but my best friend was white. Ironically, his name was Danny White.

For all intents and purposes, we were Americans—not African Americans, not blacks. The color of our skin was a non-issue and continued that way through junior high and high school and even during my early days in the workforce. I went to work at Sears-Roebuck and Co. a few months after my sixteenth birthday.

Despite my surroundings, despite the fact that all my friends were white and I had this sense that I was just an American, the same self-awareness I carry with me today—the images of the civil rights movement, King, and the struggles during that time; the moral obligation of civil disobedience combined with my mother's battle against segregation in housing—was planted in the core of my consciousness.

My parents—especially Mom, despite her own swipe at the injustice of the status quo—viewed my early resistance to unfair or unequally applied rules, as nothing more than rebellion. Keep your head down, play by the rules. That was it.

Mom was beside herself when I did the opposite.

CHAPTER 6

Signs

"Keep an eye on Kathy during the video conference call. I want to ask you something about her later."

After the call, Liz asked if I'd noticed how Kathy, her HR manager, had slumped down in her chair. "It looked as if she were sleeping and not paying attention," Liz said. "I've coached her about this several times. Her body language gives the impression that she's not interested. I'm concerned how she's perceived by upper management. If she can't fix that, I don't think she has a future with the company."

In my head, I thought, *Oh, my God, really? You are going to judge someone based on how they sit? What about her performance?* Aloud, I asked, "Does she do a decent job?" Liz didn't answer, responding instead with a question of her own. "So you think I'm making too big an issue of it then?" "Yes," I answered. *Duh!* I thought.

The Liz I'd used to know couldn't care less about something so trivial. At least not to the extent that it determined whether an employee had a future with the company. It was off the charts in relation to the quality of the work criterion. I should have realized something was up. However, I ignored this first sign that Liz had changed.

In the months to come, as the signs turned to road maps, I couldn't ignore what was obvious.

She was indifferent when I told her about those general managers who'd told me I sound like "a white guy with a stick up his ass." The Liz I knew, the Hammer, would have been all over that.

When I reported that a sales director ended Ali's candidacy for a district sales manager position out of concern that a Muslim wouldn't be acceptable to white business owners and managers in southern Virginia, she didn't investigate.

She insisted I needed documented proof that a district sales manager in Waterbury, Connecticut, rejected a candidate for a territory sales position because of his age.

She did nothing after I provided her with documentation proving the director of sales in another region, discriminated against several women, an African American, and a candidate in his fifties, choosing to hire a white male who was the least qualified. At the very least, it warranted a conversation.

To some extent, I understood her reluctance in some of these cases.

Once upon a time, during our employment at Kprints, she'd explained to me the paradigm that vexed her.

It seemed whenever a manager wasn't in good standing with the company, based strictly on profit and sales performance, the powers that be were quick to nail that manager to the wall for any wrongdoing. However, if the manager was in good standing, delivering those profits and sales, an excuse was made for any wrongdoing.

She'd noted one case where the company had covered for a manager, even though there were witnesses. It was one of those times when she'd sought my counsel. As she told it, a general store manager in Minnesota had insisted his employees participate in Saturday morale-boosting outings on their own time. During one of these outings, he took them out on the lake in his boat. As they passed one area of the beach, he noted, "That's where the God-damned zipperheads have taken over." ("Zipperheads" is a derogatory term for people of Asian descent.)

One of the employees in the boat was married to an Asian American. She and another employee took offense to the description. They both registered complaints. In addition to the violation of the zero-tolerance policy against discrimination and a hostile work environment, the manager had violated expense policy, as well as wage and hour laws.

Despite Liz's recommendation of termination, the manager, who was a top performer, was only given a slap on the wrist. Liz argued against the decision and also received a slap on the wrist for being so argumentative. She was taken aback when that incident was the basis for some criticism she received during her performance review.

I contend that it was instances like this that derailed her ascension at Kprints and thereby caused her to be cautious about confronting managers who were considered top performers at Uniforms.

Indeed, all the managers I complained about at Uniforms were in good standing. As a matter of fact, that director who saw fit to hire the least qualified applicant simply because he looked like him ended up getting promoted within a few months after I provided Liz with that proof.

My concern rose to the level of alarm in June of 2009 when Liz herself practiced discrimination. A candidate for a human resource representative position went through three interviews before she spoke with Liz. At that stage, Liz was just a rubber stamp. The decision to make an offer had already been made, save Liz's approval. She didn't give it.

Liz was concerned the candidate would expose discrimination within the company to outside agencies. Her fear was based on the fact that the candidate disclosed to her that she had filed a discrimination complaint against her last employer. It was one of the reasons she was in the job market. Liz explained her decision to pass on the candidate like this. "With all the shit the general manager [at the location the candidate would be assigned] pulls up there, we will be dealing with the EEOC forever. He's an HR nightmare."

Despite my disillusionment, I was still advising others within human resources to go directly to Liz if they weren't getting support. I was still telling people that she would do the right thing. One of those people, Melissa, a human resource representative in South Carolina, was reluctant to take that step. She also asked me not to say anything. However, the situation confronting her was so outrageous, I decided to go to Liz anyway.

Melissa registered a complaint of a hostile work environment. Kathy, despite her new regional HR director title, apparently didn't have a clue what the significance or responsibilities of that title entailed. She traveled to Melissa's location to conduct an investigation of Melissa's complaint against her general manager, Richard, but ended up investigating Melissa instead. After Kathy talked to the general manager and a few other supervisors who followed his lead, she went into Melissa's office and said, "You are the problem, not him. And, to be frank, I no longer have any confidence that you can do the job. Liz feels the same way!"

Here's the thing, and it's HR 101. Even if the person who filed the complaint has performance issues, you don't, during the course of the investigation, accuse the accuser. You certainly do not write the accuser up. And you don't threaten termination, as Kathy did. You don't change the accuser's job duties to diminish her effectiveness, as ultimately happened in this case. You don't tell her she no longer has the right to report problems within the location to anyone besides her GM, the person she accused of perpetrating the hostile work environment.

I called Liz because I couldn't believe that she condoned the use of her name the way Kathy used it, and that she would condone the write-up on Melissa or the change in her work duties. These were all classic retaliatory acts that put the company at risk—not to mention they were wrong!

Liz jumped down my throat. "What are you doing talking to her? You shouldn't be involved. You don't know all the problems we've had with her! You need to stay out of other people's business!"

Melissa talked to me as other rank-and-file employees did because the problems they encountered often involved recruiting. At least that's what I told Liz in order to calm her down. Then I mentioned recent comments by Jennie, the senior vice president of human resources. During an HR conference call with the entire HR field staff, she'd said, "I know it's difficult out there. So if you don't feel you can talk to your immediate supervisor, try to talk to someone." Melissa and others didn't think they could talk to their immediate supervisor, the general manager. And, they didn't believe they could talk to Kathy who was a dotted-line supervisor. Some of them viewed Kathy as so incompetent they'd spent time on the internet trying to find out exactly where she had received her HR training.

I was finally able to calm Liz by pointing out that Kathy, by invoking Liz's name, put her at risk. Liz was adamant that she didn't authorize Kathy to make the statement that she had lost confidence in Melissa's ability to do the job. However, the way she flew off the handle and attacked my participation told me differently. Attack-the-accuser was the plan going into the investigation. Barring undeniable evidence and collaborating witnesses to the abuse the GM had bestowed on Melissa and other women, Liz planned to support him. Kathy wasn't complicit, Liz was. It was Liz's plan all along. It was evident in her voice and her incredulous and defensive posture.

The three-way phone call between Liz, me, and Kathy confirmed that, as well. A memorandum she sent out later that day illustrated the extent of the conspiracy to cover up.

Liz and the director of employee relations at corporate devised a plan where Kathy would reach out to Melissa in a casual way. If she voiced any dissatisfaction with what happened, Kathy would refer the matter to corporate. "That way," Liz said, "we can at least show we provided an alternative source for her to talk to."

Another part of the memo referenced me. "It might be a good idea to keep Brian out of this. We wouldn't want Melissa to know he violated her confidence." It clearly gave the impression they thought I was on their side. And I guess that's what I wanted them to think. I'd already called Melissa immediately after the confrontation with Liz. I'd apologized and told her every detail of the conversation. I'd also sent Melissa the memo to keep as evidence of the conspiracy and offered to be a witness if she wanted to file a hostile workplace complaint with the EEOC.

Within a few days, I made a series of calls to other human resource representatives and operations and sales personnel in the field, including the regional HR director in the North, Arthur. He received a special apology and a warning. I'd recruited Arthur and we'd become friends. I'd shared his pain over the lack of respect and support he received from Liz. I had to apologize for not sharing the fact that she'd told me on a number of occasions about her dissatisfaction with him, and that it had reached the point where he was on the chopping block. It was my attempt to honor confidences on both sides.

Instead, I'd tried to coach him on how to deal with Liz and get on her good side. Now, by telling him everything, including the fact that Liz had shared confidential information about his performance issues, I hoped to erase the praise and statements of trust I'd bestowed on Liz that may have given Arthur a false sense of security.

For the others I contacted, it was just an apology. I had to admit that I'd been wrong when I'd told them Liz deserved their trust and that they should go to her. I took back the statement I'd made time and time again to anyone who'd complained about her or voiced an opinion that she was untrustworthy, unreasonable, and power hungry. I'd used to say, "You just need to know the other side of her. Then you would realize the solid person she is and that she can be trusted to do the right thing."

CHAPTER 7

Shitty

Corporate America is full of assholes. Robert I. Sutton, PhD, wrote a book about it. Aptly titled *The No Asshole Rule*, the book provides this description: "Assholes are people who demean and damage others."

I have met a number of these people over the years. I discuss a few of them throughout this book, however, none comes close to the regional vice president at Uniforms, Shitty. The difference between him and others comes down to motivation. Shitty is a hater. Clues to his attitudes were revealed through his invocation of his political views. I will not be surprised if, during the course of my discrimination lawsuit, we find that he is part of that Tea Party faction that is clearly up in arms for no other reason than the fact that the president is African American. Incidentally, that is only partly conjectured. On at least two occasions he referenced his disdain for president Obama. In one of those instances, he was overheard discussing the liberal agenda on taxes during those first two years of Obama's presidency. He didn't just say "liberal president and taxes" as some of my conservative friends do. He said "liberal black president and his damn tax-the-rich agenda."

Shitty and assholes like him have the additional traits of arrogance and stupidity. In his case, he was dumb enough to share his troubles with a casual acquaintance, whom, I can only assume, he believed shared his views simply because they shared the same skin color.

In January of 2009, Shitty called his friend Peter, a district manager in Florida. Shitty started the conversation by telling Peter about the rough weekend he'd had with executives at corporate in his efforts to save his promotion to regional vice president. According to Peter, an investigation into a complaint by a branch manager at one of the locations Shitty managed led to a wider investigation at two others. The discrimination, intimidation, and harassment charge by that branch manager was substantiated by like incidents at the main location in Tampa.

Shitty targeted Hispanics, African Americans, and older workers for elimination. According to witnesses, after Shitty was told by HR he couldn't just fire a Hispanic worker, he instructed the worker's supervisor to send the employee home for the day under the guise that there wasn't enough work. The employee was told he'd be called when he was needed. The plan was to let three days go by. On the fourth day, Shitty would claim the worker was a no call/no show. Under company policy, that would mean immediate termination. When the Hispanic supervisor who worked under Shitty complained about the tactic to human resources, Shitty retaliated at performance review time.

The incident that started the investigation concerned Shitty's instructions to that branch manager. Shitty had ordered him to demote and otherwise change the working conditions of several older route drivers so they would quit. The branch manager initially refused but, after pressure from Shitty, did what he was told. Because of his initial resistance and the time it took for him to move those older workers out, Shitty turned on the branch manager and eventually drove him out too.

According to Peter, Shitty's promotion was rescinded as a result of the investigation. However, he'd spent the weekend convincing those Shitty described as "idiots at corporate" that the accusations were nothing more than sour grapes over his expectation that employees perform at a higher level. Shitty was happy to report that his campaign had worked. His promotion was going through as planned, with one caveat. He wouldn't get the regional vice president title right away. He was on probation.

Shitty damned human resources, including Liz, for the trouble. She'd conducted the investigation and agreed with the executive vice president of human resources who'd recommended the action against Shitty.

Within a few months after his promotion, Shitty was up to his asshole ways again. Only this time, as a regional vice president, he had an entire region of people to demean and damage. He started with the director of sales, Edward, by undermining his ability to effectively do his job.

There's no way of knowing whether I would have conducted myself differently if I had been aware of Shitty's past.

Maybe I would have been more prepared for the negative reaction or taken extra steps to gather evidence so that when the time came to confront the discriminatory culture, the company would have to take action to correct it. But I doubt it. The fact is, he was just one of a long list of assholes in the company. There were so many like him—willing to discriminate, intimidate, violate the law, and cover up—that I was convinced I had to confront the problem head-on. Because the thing is, the company knew about these assholes, just like they knew about Shitty, and they covered for them.

I read a news story in May of 2011 that not only highlighted the tactics of one of the assholes, it also demonstrated the lengths the company went to in order to cover for him.

A jury awarded former Uniforms employee Drew $261,000. The award included $200,000 in punitive damages, as the jury determined the employee's workers' compensation claim was a "motivating factor" in his termination.

According to the complaint, retaliation against the employee included negative comments by a production supervisor stating the employee was faking his injury. A manager allegedly said the employee was "out to cause trouble," and other employees threatened physical harm. According to the lawsuit, the employee reported the threats to management on at least three different occasions. Within three months, they found a way to terminate him. According to management, he'd made "multiple false representations" about his medical history during his pre-employment physical exam in 2008.

I wasn't there, but based on my own experience and that of others when I was in the loop, it isn't difficult to imagine what happened.

In this case, the motivation was about money—plain and simple. Drew had sustained an injury on the job and, therefore, needed assistance to do his job. And here's how it probably played out:

His asshole manager, upset over the additional labor costs, begins to talk negatively about the employee. Soon, others who are genuinely upset because the manager has put it in their minds that Drew isn't pulling his weight, start to threaten him. The on-site HR representative is brought in, based on the claim that Drew is faking his injury. Drew complains about the treatment he is receiving. The asshole manager labels him a troublemaker. The HR representative escalates the situation to the regional HR director who, after consulting corporate human resources, then finds a way to carry out the manager's desire to terminate the employee. In the meantime, additional punitive action is implemented, taking away the assistance given the employee to accommodate his disability. This action, along with the creation of a hostile environment, is designed to force the employee to quit.

In Houston, Texas, HR representative Tina told me about the asshole she was dealing with. She reported harassment by her general manager when she'd called in sick and then took a leave of absence. Her EEOC complaint alleged the termination was due to age, race, and retaliation for exercising her rights under FMLA (Family Medical Leave Act).

In Tampa, Florida, the asshole was the general manager, as well. Phil was fond of telling employees he would crush them. He bragged to me personally about how he manipulated the system in order to carry out his threats to eliminate employees he didn't like.

A branch manager who reported to the general manager would later admit he'd helped ruin careers at the behest of the general manager. Another employee would eventually file a complaint alleging threats of termination if he sought medical treatment for a shoulder injury he suffered while on the job. He would eventually seek medical treatment on his own time and at his own expense. The surgery performed required him to take time off from work. But his fear of retaliation forced him back to work where he reinjured the shoulder and was unable to perform his duties at the level expected. He was forced out. He never received an answer to the complaint he filed with the company, so he decided to go to the EEOC.

He would tell me how the general manager operated through intimidation and fear. In addition, there were instances of discrimination. In one case, the GM refused to allow the employee to hire a candidate for a route service position because "he was black and bug-eyed."

That same GM bragged about his plans to force out a "seasoned" district manager. When that district manager was replaced with an employee who was considerably younger—with considerably less experience and a performance record that didn't come close to matching his—he filed an age discrimination complaint.

In Louisville, Kentucky, the asshole general manager convinced his human resource representative Ken to withhold information from the regional human resource director regarding a negative accident report they'd received on one of their drivers. The GM wanted time to work something out. He knew that Kathy would make him follow policy and procedure and terminate the driver immediately. After a few weeks, Kathy was at the location and questioned why she hadn't been brought into the loop sooner. The general manager looked at Ken and said, "Yeah, Ken, why didn't you report this to Kathy right away? You know that's the procedure." Ken took the blame. When it came out later that the general manager was the one who'd given those instructions, Ken was retaliated against.

One of the things that caused trouble for Karen, the HR representative at the New Jersey location was her Puerto Rican heritage and fluency in Spanish. Early in my employment, the asshole general manager complained to me about Karen's relationship with the Hispanic workers in the plant. "She's always speaking in Spanish with them," he claimed, "and she tends to side with them." He insinuated she was conspiring with the Hispanic workers against management instead of on behalf of management. To make his case he would explain how all the Hispanic employees went to her about their issues—from working conditions to needing time off—instead of their immediate supervisors. He overlooked the fact that the supervisors didn't speak Spanish.

One of the reasons Karen had been hired for the job was because she was bilingual. Karen believed she was simply doing her job as a translator for the employees. She was also doing her job when she challenged the service manager for wanting to disqualify job applicants whom he classified as too old or "too Hispanic." When she contacted her HR director for advice on how to deal with employee relations issues, she was following standard protocol. But it wasn't a surprise to her when the general manager attempted to create new rules and guidelines to limit her access to employees and contain information about what was going on at the location.

Among other things, Karen wasn't allowed to speak to Hispanic employees without their supervisors present. When she toured the plant floor, which was a regular requirement of the job as part of the employee relations and safety review process, she had to be accompanied by a supervisor, as well. According to Karen, the general manager confronted her directly, insisting that she keep everything inside the location and challenging her decision to tell Liz the truth about certain negative situations that prevailed.

When a new general manager took over the location, the situation got worse for Karen. She would later allege that this is when the retaliation that ultimately forced her to seek other employment began. The company conducted a time study after reducing her workload. The study determined she didn't have enough to do, giving the company cause to add clerical work to her duties. It was a change that diminished the quality of her job. Other employees who were in the loop would tell her about the company's general negative perception of her and their uncertainty whether she could be trusted as a member of the core management team. Negative talk about her performance escalated when she provided me with information directly related to my discrimination and retaliation complaint in June of 2010.

I'd had my own confrontations with many of these same managers. It wasn't difficult to believe or take the side of employees who related their situations to me and sought my advice. When Karen told me how her first general manager had called a meeting with his management team and coached them on what to say and how to act during a planned visit by the senior vice president of operations, I wasn't surprised. He instructed them to leave out any negatives about the business and to focus instead on all the positive aspects. It was in line with the warning he'd given me the first time I'd met him, that any issues or concerns involving him or his business units needed to stay in the confines of our relationship. He'd said, "We all have our own way of doing things, and you'll find life can be difficult if you're one of those people who believes the open environment really works."

He was one of the first managers to stop cooperating with my recruiting efforts— because I did believe in an open environment and I was open about my problems with him.

These last two assholes worked directly for Shitty. It's my belief that the quantity of assholes created the environment that turned otherwise good people, like Liz, into people like them.

Peter wouldn't relate to me the details of Shitty's dirty, racist, asshole tactics until sometime in August 2010. That was three months after I'd filed my discrimination complaint and more than seven months after Shitty had initiated the retaliation designed to demean and damage me.

CHAPTER 8

When Liz Fell

Some of the conversations captured by the mini-recorder I held to the phone and carried with me in the breast pocket of my suit jacket are muffled. However, even in those instances, it isn't hard to make out what was said. Unfortunately, the content, which could go a long way toward proving my claims of discrimination and retaliation, is only useful for the purpose of assisting my memory. In the state of Wisconsin, although it is legal to record conversations under the one-party rule, so long as the person doing the recording is one of the participants, the dialogue is not admissible as evidence in a legal proceeding.

I began recording conversations at work some time in the twelfth month of my employment when it became clear that the discrimination I witnessed was systemic and the company wasn't going to take any real action to stop it. By the time interactions between Liz and myself had turned consistently negative, prompting the following memo, recording conversations became a regular routine.

From:	Brian D Nord/UNIFORMS 08/03/2010 07:54 AM
To:	Liz /UNIFORMS
Cc:	Jennie /UNIFORMS@UNIFORMS
Subject:	Re: Action Required—Need your signed perform document

I don't know what game you think you're playing with the "I'm confused" and "don't understand" type of comments, however, I'm not playing.

You need to accept the fact that I am not signing the document under any circumstances and we need to move on and try to get the job done despite what has clearly become a hostile and difficult environment for me.

That said, since some of my concerns directly involve my EEOC complaint, I will be happy to make myself available after I have the opportunity to first review this situation with my attorney. He is out of the country until next Monday.

I have to make it clear that I don't trust anything you have to say, your motivation, or your conduct, and I will have to insist that Jennie is involved in any conversation we have in regard to this matter. And as far as I am concerned, everything is on the table, including the numerous incidents of discrimination I reported that you did nothing about and the numerous conversations where you divulged what you called confidential information.

In truth, I did understand the game Liz was playing. She was trying to protect her ass by playing ignorant about one false statement she inserted in my year end performance review which had the capacity to lay ground work for establishing future performance related issues, if I had agreed to it. I'd refused to sign the year-end appraisal. As far as I was concerned it was an additional attempt to retaliate against me for my opposition to discrimination.

The e-mail was the final nail in the coffin of my ten-year friendship with Liz.

The destruction had begun eight months earlier during a call when tempers had flared and I'd ended up hanging up on her.

It was February of 2010, three weeks before my presentation at the North managers meeting. Liz called me to discuss events from a recent executive staff meeting she'd attended at corporate. The CEO acknowledged that he agreed with the basis of a plan proposed to him by Liz and the senior director of sales, Adam. Their idea was to give field managers the option of keeping positions open in order to spend more time training existing sales staff. The belief was that the constant influx of new salespeople—and the detailed training required to prepare them—resulted in neglect in the development of existing staff and, therefore, negatively affected sales growth.

However, by February the new strategy was playing havoc with reaching monthly sales projections as managers followed the new strategy leaving sales positions open and thus failing to make sales goals.

The CEO provided the history in an attempt to explain his latest edict, which was to reverse course, going back to the original strategy. At the time, the Southern region, based on decisions not to fill positions, was down eleven headcount. I had already begun to make headway in reducing that number when Liz called me.

"You've been here for a number of months now," she said. "What would you say is the overriding reason we aren't able to build a better image of the recruiting department?" My answer: "There's no accountability or consistency."

As the regional recruiting manager, I was supposed to have the ability to interject myself into the process at any location when needed. However, most general managers preferred to rely on their local HR representative for recruiting. At locations where I was welcome, positions were filled.

This wasn't new information, and I pointed this out to Liz for the umpteenth time. When she asked what we could do to improve things, I suggested, yet again, that regional recruiting managers should be forced to do all the sales recruiting for their regions. I referred to it as a centralized process. One person responsible and one person held accountable. The only way to ensure compliance would be "if it's official company policy," I told her. "That's the only way general managers and district managers will go along. There will be accountability at all levels. More importantly, there will be no more excuses."

Incidentally, there is nothing rewarding about doing volume recruiting for the same position. I wasn't asking for something that benefited me. I would be miserable in that drudgery. But that's beside the point. The system was broken, the position was crucial, and it didn't make sense that the person with the most experience and time wasn't responsible. I restated my original argument.

As it was, failure to hire or keep positions filled could be blamed on just about anyone. General managers blamed it on their district sales managers. District sales managers blamed it on the local HR representative. The truth may have been that the general manager purposely refused to fill positions because he wanted to save on budget. The district manager held up the process because he was too busy making sales calls in those open territories. And yes, not only were human resource representatives overworked, they didn't have the recruiting experience, didn't want to recruit, and were often not allowed time to recruit.

I offered Liz proof that the centralized process would work. In the weeks leading up to this conversation, a few general managers allowed me to implement the plan at their location. They were the top locations in the regions and kept positions filled 100 percent of the time. I had even succeeded in getting a few minorities hired. Essentially, what had occurred by accident was the implementation of my centralized recruiting process.

"If we make this permanent," I said, and expand it to the entire company "you'll see the momentum continue and, at least in my regions, we'll be at 100 percent all the time."

Her response was, "That's bullshit. You should have never been down ten headcount in the first place. The only reason you're making headway now is because I got on your ass about it!"

Remember in the first chapter when I referenced the conversation I'd had that turned heated? This was it. It started with that statement. In response I blew my stack. I argued, raising my voice to a level that could easily justify a charge of insubordination. While Liz was blaming me for the lack of headcount and then taking credit for the improvement at some locations "by getting on my ass", she didn't know I had a copy of the memo from the CEO acknowledging that it was her idea to leave positions open. Although I should have thrown that memo from the CEO in her face, I didn't mention it.

Somewhere in the conversation she shouted, "Don't yell at me!" I got louder and angrier instead. "This conversation is over," she said. "You're not going to talk to me like that."

"What about my idea of centralized recruiting?" I asked.

"We're not doing that. Period. The conversation is over, I'm not going to tolerate—"

"Damn right it's over!" I screamed. Then I hung up on her.

Although we would reconcile before the end of that day and Liz may have thought the issue was closed, it wasn't. I went over her head. The same day I made the presentation to that group of managers in the North, I made the centralized recruiting argument to the senior vice president of operations. He was the decider. I went as far as telling him that he wasn't getting his money's worth out of my position. "The level of activity I'm allowed makes this a twenty-five hour a week job." I said. "I suggest that if the company doesn't want to put me to work, they'd be better off eliminating my position."

Most changes require a committee and an analysis that lasts for months. In this instance, it took less than twelve hours. The next day the VP pulled me aside. "I just got off the phone with Liz," he said, "and told her to implement your plan."

A week later, Liz rolled the new structure out to field HR on a conference call saying, "Adam and I have been thinking about this for a long time. We have put a lot of thought into it. The company has decided to go along with our idea of centralizing the recruiting process."

The calls I received from the field were endless the rest of that day. HR directors Terri and Arthur, human resource reps, and sales and operations all chimed in. The theme was the same. "Really, she took credit for your idea? Wasn't she against it? Can you believe that—now it's her idea?" There was even a "Wow!" in there somewhere, a "What do you think of her now?" and at least three, "I told you so."

Liz destroyed her credibility with everyone who had prior knowledge. I had been consulting with people all along attempting to get their buy-in and support for months.

I could describe these incidents as the last straw, but what finally ended our relationship was also the worst of her betrayal—so deep it would have been less damaging if she had stabbed me in the back with a serrated knife and twisted it over and over again—also eventually led to my EEOC complaint, the e-mail confrontation, and a secret meeting with the sr. vp of human resources and the director of employee relations, where I would rat Liz out.

Liz turned on me when I complained about retaliation from Shitty. Liz had refused to do anything about it. Instead, she'd made excuses for him.

I was able to show a clear pattern of behavior that defied any of the excuses she made for him. It made no business sense to give a contract recruiter access to hiring managers that I didn't have. It defied reason to invite that outside recruiter to a conference call on recruiting and leave me out.

There was no logic to keeping me from other regional meetings or ignoring my requests for information on recruiting goals. However, all these actions were logical if the plan was to undermine my efforts to do the job and thus create a performance issue that could be acted upon.

The excommunication and other methods used to undermine my ability to do my job got to the point where the outside recruiter had so much more information, he was informing me of recruiting assignments. I provided Liz e-mails as proof. It was enough for her to address the most pressing issue I brought up: Shitty was a racist asshole who couldn't deal with the black guy who'd told that room full of white guys that they discriminated and it had to stop.

In April, as the retaliation escalated I refused to take her "no" to requests for action as an answer. I provided Liz with documented proof that Shitty was avoiding me altogether and refused to cooperate. I demanded an investigation. "He's a racist," I told her. I also requested reassignment to another region.

Finally, she intervened. However, even then, she never confronted him on the fundamental aspects of my complaint. She simply announced my removal from the region. By her own account, Shitty trashed my performance during the conversation. She offered no rebuttal, even though she had proof to the contrary. The Hammer would have used the "duck is a duck" statement.

When I told my friend Meg about the latest events, she interrupted when I made comments about how the change in Liz was testament to how truly corrupt the environment at Uniforms was. "She turned to the dark side, damning a ten-year friendship and everything it was based on," I said.

"It wasn't a change in her at all!" Meg insisted. "She took credit for your idea. She threw you under the bus! I remember another time when she took credit for something someone else did." Then she reminded me of an incident from our Kprints days.

Earlier in the book I mentioned how Liz broke company rules when it came to downsizing and kept me on the payroll. A few years later, I was telling that story during a gathering at the corporate headquarters in Dallas. I pointed to Liz as I ended, making the final point that she was a quality manager.

She was looking over my shoulder and said, "Actually, I wasn't the one who decided to keep you back then. Sean made that decision." As I turned to see what she was looking at, Sean, who had been promoted to vice president of human resources by then, was standing there. Later that day, Sean asked, "What was that all about?" He'd only heard the tail end of my comments and what Liz had said.

I told him I was shocked when Liz made that statement because she had heard me tell that story a number of times in the past and never corrected me. Sean laughed. Then he confirmed that he made the call about keeping me on the payroll. Liz, he said, had insisted that I needed to go based on policy.

Being reminded of that event forced me finally to admit that Meg and others were right all along. Yet, even today I hold on to the belief that the complete destruction of her character was more a reflection of the insidiousness of the Uniforms culture than of her. She is but one example of many who are taken in by the system and thus corrupted.

There can be no claim of virtue in only following one's conscience and morals when it's convenient, void of risk or controversy. But if the corrupt culture we'd found ourselves in had been the opposite, Liz would not have changed. As it was, just as I had to resort to some of the underhanded things I did to help job applicants to survive, people like Liz are forced to adjust—and even abandon their morals and ethics to survive.

Liz's refusal to confront the discrimination with Shitty, left me no choice but to take my complaints outside the company and file charges with the EEOC.

On August 9, 2010. Jennie, Uniforms senior vice president of human resources, and Curtis, the director of employee relations, flew to Milwaukee, Wisconsin, to meet with me in confidence, to discuss the memo and all the events that led up to it. Even though I began the meeting by denying I was recording the conversation, when Jennie asked, it was on the entire time.

The meeting lasted two hours. Five days later, Liz was no longer with the company.

CHAPTER 9

Dirty Stuff Going On

A fifty-three-year-old executive recruiter named Nick who has worked for leading U.S. staffing firms since 1990 went on record with a reporter Laura Bassett in the January 14, 2011, edition of the *Huffington Post*. Bassett wrote, "As an industry insider, he became privy to the many ways companies and staffing firms sidestep labor laws. "There's a lot of dirty stuff going on, a lot of hush-hush discrimination, I can assure you. As a recruiter, you get a HR director on the phone, and they tell you point blank, 'We want somebody in this age bracket, or this particular gender, currently has a job. We don't want to see a resume from anyone who is not working.' It happens all the time."

Reading the whole of the information provided by Nick, you get the impression that although he was appalled by the practice, he went along.

Going along is one alternative a recruiter has to avoid suffering the retaliation I endured.

In general, recruiters go along for a variety of reasons. Ignorance is one part of it, especially for rookies; they simply don't know the discrimination laws. Fear of retaliation plays a role, but just as often many recruiters are in lockstep with the discriminatory bias.

Beyond that, if it's an outside recruiter on contract—including the staffing companies Nick worked for—it's all about money. If a staffing company doesn't adhere to a client's request, refusing to go along or by sending candidates solely based on qualifications, the client has other staffing companies lined up to provide applicants. And many of those staffing companies are more than willing to meet any demand.

The collusion is varied, widespread, and voluntary, without a client company or hiring manager saying a word. It doesn't take long for a recruiter to figure out what's going on because after a while a pattern emerges. It becomes clear that a particular company or hiring manager is only going to hire someone of a certain age, gender, or race. Once a recruiter figures that out, he or she screens candidates to meet that requirement, even if the client company did not specifically request it.

In July of 2011, a friend of mine who lives in Florida sought me out for job-search advice. James had experience in the recruiting industry but had been out of it since the mid-'90s. For the past fifteen years, he'd worked for the same company in advertising sales. He was skeptical when I told him there was a need to summarize experience that went beyond fifteen years and eliminate dates on his education, which would enable prospective employers to calculate his age.

Two months later, when he called to give me an update on his progress, he told me about the interaction he'd had with four different headhunters. Three of them were quick to ask questions that would allow them to verify his age. One asked what year he'd graduated from college. Another wanted to know what year he'd graduated from high school. The third asked him how many years of work experience he'd had prior to the last job shown on his resume. Until that third contact, James answered truthfully, allowing them to estimate his age at fifty-six.

The first two interviews ended abruptly after he'd answered. Both recruiters left him with the impression they were going to call back to schedule an interview date with the employer. They never did. When he got the third call, he took a cue from another *Huffington Post* article I'd sent him from March 1, 2011.

One of the people highlighted in the story was a woman by the name of Ruth, a fifty-nine-year-old born on April 28, 1951. The reporter wrote, "After two and a half years of not even being able to get an interview for a job, she decided that her new "job application birth date" was going to be March 19, 1969. 'They're asking for your Social Security number and date of birth on applications now, which I don't think they have a right to do unless they're hiring you, and you don't have the option of not filling them in," she told a reporter. 'You either fill them in right or you lie, and I'm all for lying.' As Ruth tells it, she received an interview with the very next application using her new birth date, and she got the job.

James decided to lie, as well. He told the next headhunter he had no work history prior to 1988. That allowed the headhunter to estimate his age to be forty-four, after taking into account graduating from high school and four years of college. The call advanced to the stage where the headhunter provided in-depth information about a company seeking applicants and prepped James for the interview that the recruiter all but guaranteed would occur within the next week. Sure enough, within a few days, James had a video-conference interview with the CEO and a division president of an international company. Whether any of those recruiters were directly told by their clients that age was an issue or they figured it out themselves, their tactics violated the law.

This next story ran in the *Huffington Post* on August 11, 2011.

"Some staffing firms, when questioned by reporters, are up front about their intention to recruit only people who currently have jobs. Martin Recruiting Partners, a restaurant staffing agency based in Georgia, ran ads which stated candidates 'Must be currently working and ready to move for the right reason.'

"George Seed, the company's vice president of operations, defended the policy. 'When my clients hire me, they want people who are motivated to go to work for the right reasons,' Seed said. 'And if someone is currently employed in a good position, then their motivation to move to a different company would be that the company offers better benefits or offers more growth for advancement, or whatever. They're not people who have to have a job, they're people who want to move for the right reasons.'

"Seed, along with representatives from four other staffing agencies listed in [a] NELP [National Employment Law Project] report, said many of his clients only consider job applicants who are presently employed and they claimed those clients requested the language."

Another recruiter made this statement on National Public Radio (NPR) on November 17, 2010: "If you think about the talent in that unemployed market, you would realize that companies rarely lay off their best skilled workers...It's people that aren't top performers. So if you're ABC Corporation and you're trying to hire the best salesperson out there, and you're looking at unemployed people, it might not be the group of people with the best skills."

This outrageous mindset was echoed in yet another story in the *Huffington Post* around the same time. A headhunter defended the practice of disqualifying the unemployed, stating in so many words that employed individuals are the gold standard. There has to be something wrong with someone who is unemployed, the headhunter reasoned, because if the employee were a top performer, the company would never have let him or her go in the first place.

Either these recruiters don't genuinely believe what they are saying and are just attempting to do PR, or they believe that crap, which means they aren't very bright. Anyone who has been involved in recruiting for any period of time knows full well that unemployed people are just as motivated, if not more motivated, than someone who is currently working. Not only are they motivated to get the job, but once they do land the position they work their asses off to limit the possibility they will become unemployed again. Those recruiters also know that since the early '90s, with outsourcing, downsizing, mergers, and acquisitions, a lot of those unemployed people lost their jobs regardless of whether they were a top performer or not. Whole companies went under, entire divisions or position categories were eliminated. It's a numbers game—period.

In addition, the fact that someone is employed doesn't automatically mean they are a top performer. It's just as likely the worker's greatest skill is nothing more than kissing ass or keeping his or her head down. It's just as likely the person simply knows how to play politics.

In 2009, as Uniforms fought to limit the toll of the economic downturn, they executed a reorganization that included downsizing.

During this period, Doug, the vice president of field human resources, was involved in a special project because of his vast experience. It took him away from his day-to-day duties, so he assigned my boss and friend Liz to fill in for him. To put it mildly, Doug is one of the most solid HR professionals I have ever met during my thirty-plus years in the workforce. I make that evaluation from the perspective of having held jobs over the length of my career in sales, management, director level personnel, and director and executive level recruiting. I've had dealings with other executives at all levels, including CEOs and boards of directors of multibillion dollar companies. That experience included the likes of Sears, A&P, Federal Express, and Michaels, to name a few. That interaction provided an in-depth understanding of what a top notch manager was.

While Doug tended to the special project, Liz, by her own admission, on a number of occasions undercut and undermined several policies, ideas, and initiatives he'd put into place. She told me how she knew that Doug and the executive vice president of human resources, Jennie, didn't always see eye to eye. She was going to make sure she came down on the side of the executive VP at every opportunity. I never thought anything of it at the time, attributing it to the open environment with the core policy of speaking out and challenging.

When the announced cuts came, which included human resources, Doug, despite his experience that far exceeded Liz's, was out. Although they reduced the title to senior director level, she got his job.

I still didn't fully grasp how Liz had maneuvered her way into Doug's job until she, without realizing it, spelled it out. And, for all I know, based on other incidents I would become privy to as time went on, Jennie may have been more than happy to jettison Doug. The word in the field was that he had a much better rapport with field management, and they didn't care for Jennie much. Doug was certainly a top performer and a straight shooter, and she may have considered him a threat.

Ironically, Liz-herself, was on the short end of a similar situation. Years earlier at Kprints, Liz was the stronger of two regional HR directors. Yet, the other director—who, among other things, had shown too much of a willingness to cater to the whims of operations when it came to inappropriate classification of minorities and women—was chosen over Liz to fill one of two newly created senior director level positions. He got the job for no other reason than his status as a member of the "good old boys" network. It certainly wasn't because he was more qualified.

This kind of behavior occurs every day in corporate America. So the idea that a job applicant who is employed automatically qualifies as the gold standard is bunk. Any recruiter who uses that reasoning to justify discriminating against the unemployed is an idiot or is simply trying to maintain favor with the employment marketplace and limit his or her culpability.

I make this point to debunk the general perception that recruiters are on the side of job applicants. They are not! Recruiters go along with all kinds of dirty stuff because the alternative is retaliation. They go along because they are afraid not to and can't afford job loss. They—we—cannot be trusted.

CHAPTER 10

Anything Goes

This item appeared in a story on August 7, 2003, in the UK's *Manchester Evening News*.

"A man who had applied for hundreds of jobs was told not to mention a disability to prospective employers, as it could prevent him from getting work. Unemployed Paul W. claimed a career counselor told him he would have a better chance if he left all mention of his disability off job applications and forms. For the same reasons, I was also told to avoid any mention of the industrial accident I had. When I put it to them that an employer would be sure to question why I hadn't worked for so long, they just told me to make a few things up."

Another job applicant reported that he was told to "dumb down his education if he wanted to get a job."

The career counselors and a spokesperson for the staffing firm denied telling job applicants to do anything but tell the truth.

Recruiters will not admit coaching job applicants, any more than they will admit going along with discrimination. The risk is too great, regardless of which side they are on.

Even when I was confronted with the evidence that I coached a job applicant in violation of company policy, I vehemently denied it. So I guess this could be called my coming out. I confess that I have, throughout my career, coached job applicants in every conceivable way, whenever necessary.

Coaching job applicants in the way Paul was is the alternative to going along with discrimination. It is the alternative to challenging managers who discriminate or calling out a culture of discrimination and thereby risking the job-ending retaliation that comes with it.

At some point, I drew a line in the sand. I started fooling those hiring managers and the companies I worked for. Some people have described it as working undercover for job applicants. I describe it as working underground.

There is an automatic trust that comes with a recruiter position—an unspoken understanding of confidentiality with the hiring manager. As one of them put it, "You're one of us, so I can tell you."

It has always been disturbing to me how hiring managers automatically assume that, despite the color of my skin, I'll understand and go along with negative stereotypical comments they make about my race, not to mention what they say about others. Maybe they are just stupid. Maybe it's because they are so used to talking out loud that way they can't help it. Or maybe it is because they know they have the tools of a retaliatory culture to weed me out if I refuse to go along. Whatever their reasoning, when I am able to keep my cool I allow them to speak openly to give the illusion that I am indeed one of them and willing to go along. When there's evidence of an unfair corporate system—either through lack of action against those who discriminate or sheer denial despite discrimination staring them in the face (like a meeting room filled with a hundred or so white male managers)—I go underground.

I take advantage of that trust. While hiring managers expect me to lie to job applicants by withholding the true reasons they were eliminated from consideration, I tell the applicant the truth.

My rule is straightforward: anything goes. If I lie, it is to hiring managers and the companies I work for. If I cover up, it is for job applicants.

As mentioned earlier, many managers are covert about their activity, but eventually that pattern will emerge. Once I figure out the lay of land, I use the information to help job applicants beat whatever unfair system exists. I will provide them with whatever information and cover they need to keep them from being unfairly weeded out.

The question that has plagued me my entire career is whether I made the switch from loyal employee to job-applicant advocate soon enough.

Despite the series of discriminatory cultures I found myself in—which would suggest I needed to assume each new employer would be no better than the last and go underground immediately—there were times when I waited. I felt an obligation to give the system a chance.

I have consistently waited, preferring to work within whatever established system existed. I followed protocol to address any kind of discrimination or unfair treatment of job applicants.

At best, I may have had the freedom to confront a manager at the time of the incident, but more often I was limited to simply reporting the incident and leaving it to someone who had the authority and responsibility to investigate.

That's the way I played it at Uniforms.

The "dirty stuff" began to materialize within a few weeks of my employment, just as it had at Kprints and other companies I'd worked for. But a little over a year went by before I did anything beyond the aforementioned working within the system.

I felt an additional obligation to give the Uniforms system the benefit of the doubt because of my relationship with my boss Liz. She'd brought me in. Because of our association, the last thing I wanted was to do anything that would reflect badly on her. The corporate environment being what it is, antiestablishment behavior by one individual has the potential to reflect negatively on others. I did not want to risk tarnishing her rising star. Besides that, there were promises made, and I had to give her and, therefore, the system the benefit of the doubt. She assured me the company was "all in" when it came to inclusion and diversity. Beyond that understanding was the loyalty of friendship factor. The ten years we'd known each other meant something to me.

Incidentally, in this instance it was Liz, by her lack of action when I reported discrimination, who turned me from loyal employee to job-applicant advocate.

When I provided the newspaper story about Ruth to my friend James, it was more than just about giving him an example of what it might take to get fair treatment. I cheered her actions with admiration. Ruth had reasonably come to the conclusion that she was being excluded because of her age and decided that she wasn't going to be a victim anymore. She decided to break the rules by lying—in essence to fight fire with fire. It was an "if companies aren't going to follow the rules, then neither am I" kind of attitude. I cheered because she'd figured out on her own what so many others like Paul haven't: the rules are not the rules. It depends on who you are, whom you know, or what you look like. She figured out that the only rule that companies and the managers who work for them go by is anything goes.

Just as she lied for herself, I have lied for job applicants and helped them to lie. There are no company rules, standards, or confidences I will not violate in the name of fairness.

If I were one of those career counselors who'd advised Paul, I would have given him specific instructions on what to "make up" to disguise the fact that he had not worked for so long. There were times when I actually provided applicants with a job title, dates of employment, and a company name to put on their resumes and talk about during a job interview.

In late 1996, when it looked like the discrimination at FSfoods was going to go on unabated, I registered a company, National Associates, for the dual purpose of establishing a new staffing firm and providing an official company for job applicants to use as a reference.

The idea, even back then, was to eliminate the excuse of unemployment to disguise discrimination for other reasons. In today's job climate, it has become even more relevant, with companies expanding their legal but discriminatory, "must be currently employed" standard to all job applicants.

Depending on the depth of deception within a company, I didn't care about any established standard beyond whether the applicant had verifiable experience in the job they were being considered for—not when there was a double standard holding one applicant to the exact requirements while being flexible with others depending on their age, gender, or race. If I wanted everyone to be treated equally, I couldn't care about something as insignificant as whether a candidate supervised five people as a manager instead of the minimum standard of eight. I couldn't care what your grade point average was or even if you'd had a felony conviction. Since double standards were used to disguise discrimination, I was forced to find my own loopholes in the system to get the job applicant to the next level.

As terribly unethical as all this might seem, in my estimation it was nothing compared to the unethical and illegal conduct perpetrated by hiring managers and companies in general.

The reason that career counselor advised Paul to leave off his disability when filling out applications was because companies fear such people. They are willing to weed them out, in violation of the law, rather than take the risk that a disabled applicant might be less productive and, therefore, cost them money.

Money was the reason Paul was advised not to mention the industrial accident or his workers' compensation. Companies are automatically skeptical about claims of actual injuries. They hold in their minds the limited example of employees who've faked it or gamed the system in order to get paid without having to work. In many cases, it is an assumption that a worker who was injured once will be injured again and then cost the company money.

Being privy to that kind of strategy is the reason I insisted one applicant hide the fact that he'd had a heart attack a few years earlier. It's also why I explained to another that she needed to hide the fact that she was pregnant.

It's the same inside information Liz had pointed to when she'd explained how she'd refrained from mentioning that she had two small children when she'd applied for her job at Uniforms. Her reason for nondisclosure came from a negative incident that had occurred during her interview with a company prior to her landing at Uniforms. According to Liz, all had been going well during the face-to-face interview. The managers she interviewed with had even indicated that a job offer was imminent as they'd taken her on a tour of the corporate office. It was shortly after they'd viewed the daycare center that their attitudes seem to change.

There, the VP had mentioned the company's belief in the balance between work and personal life, and Liz had said that she had two small children. The VP had immediately dropped off the tour, directing his secretary to accompany Liz the rest of the way. Shortly thereafter, Liz was in a taxi headed for the airport. The entire ride she'd wondered why the day had ended so abruptly. After two weeks and no call-back, she determined that it had been the revelation that she had small children that had nixed her hiring. The corporate office provided daycare for corporate employees, but she surmised that a field HR director position, which required travel, was a different story. So, out of caution, she never mentioned her family again during job interviews.

It wasn't enough to just help job applicants by altering or concealing information. The strategy of anything goes extended to providing answers to interview questions, as well as tests and assessments. In 2002, I knew a hiring manager who was high on job applicants who confessed that their primary motivation was fear; I advised applicants to impress him by talking about fear of failure and fear of not being the best.

During my FSfoods days, it was a company philosophy passed down from the founder that married applicants with children were the best people. I advised single applicants to express their marriage and family plans if they weren't already in that circumstance.

These are just the highlights of a long list. My point is I used the philosophy of anything goes as the only means to help job applicants and protect myself from retaliation. I have no apologies, only regrets. I regret not doing it soon enough. I regret not doing it often enough.

Here's the thing. While some of the criteria that companies and hiring managers utilize to determine a job applicant's suitability is legal, I had to remember that it wasn't applied equally and that everyone, at every level of a company, was involved.

Here is a perfect example:

Despite the fact that the job description for a general manager position at Uniforms stated a college degree was preferred, according to Liz the powers that be insisted all future candidates had to be top-grades (have the ability to advance) and, therefore, had to have college—no exceptions. This was the reason she gave for the rejection of several candidates who happened to be minorities. Imagine my disgust when, during that period, Bob, a job applicant referred by another general manager, received an interview and was offered a general manager position despite not having a college degree. And that wasn't the worst of it. When our outside vendor conducted the background check, they reported they could not verify his high school diploma. That was putting it kindly. The actual written report from the school stated he didn't graduate. Liz's response when I made her aware of this: "Does it matter? I mean the regional VP already hired him. I think the issue is moot, so let it go."

The issue wasn't moot! Offers are contingent on the background check. The offer can be rescinded at any time.

This kind of craziness is what pushed me to go beyond just coaching job applicants. If any of my tactics failed and the job applicant's rejection was based on discrimination, I made sure to keep records that went beyond the qualifications of the individual who was hired in their stead. I recorded conversations, maintained e-mails, and tracked hiring patterns on spreadsheets.

I am not above using the information to blackmail a manager into doing the right thing or forcing a company to change their culture. The same information can be used to make a larger case against a culture of a company, as well as instances in which I was retaliated against.

Although this strategy comes with risk, it isn't as perilous as opposing managers or a culture that discriminates.

And it was far more rewarding to help job applicants get a fair and equal opportunity for the job. Despite the fact that I am always looking over my shoulder, I have to confess that I actually enjoyed this part of the game as it allowed me to do the job I was hired to do—recruit the most qualified based on nothing more than job qualifications. There is additional satisfaction knowing that, in a roundabout way, I am not only holding those managers accountable, I am holding the companies accountable to living up to their promises of inclusion and diversity, whether they like the way I go about it or not.

But make no mistake, there are risks to job applicants and people like me who help them. You read about part of it with those career counselors turned in by Paul. The reason the story ended up in the news was because he went to a local reporter.

The biggest risk is being found out and terminated if you are a recruiter or disqualified if you are a job applicant.

While hiring managers and companies are quick to lie and manufacture information in violation of their own integrity standards, they are just as quick to disqualify a candidate for any signs that point to a lack of integrity or honesty.

While there are people like Paul who believe it comes down to the question of honesty and integrity of the individual, I would argue it comes down to the honesty and integrity of the company and whether one's personal integrity is going to allow a corrupt system to keep one from making a living and taking care of one's family.

The question I ask is this: would you rather tell the truth and never have a chance at the job at all, not even an interview? Or would you rather risk being found out later, but at least have a chance?

I have had a few of my own moments where a job applicant like Paul spilled the beans. One of them led to a confrontation with a VP at Kprints who accused me of working undercover for job applicants.

An hour into the interview, the job applicant was hitting it off with a regional vice president of sales and feeling pretty comfortable. So much so that he let his guard down. The VP noted how impressed he was with one of the applicant's answers. The applicant responded by saying, "Yeah, I got that one from Brian. He told me the answer would win you over." That led to revelations of other coaching I had given him, including some changes to his resume.

When the VP confronted me, he went on and on about honesty and integrity and how I had failed to meet company standards. He accused me of working undercover for job applicants and threatened my job, telling me, "You're toast!"

The VP wasn't wrong in his assessment of my conduct or that I would indeed be toast if he turned me in, using the job applicant as evidence. However, that was a critical "if" because I pointed out that he couldn't hurt me without hurting himself.

I would describe my rebuttal to his admonishment as blackmail. I reminded him of the coaching I'd given him when he'd first applied to Kprints, as well as the coaching he'd requested to prepare for the interview that had resulted in his promotion to the VP position he now held. I let him know that I still had copies of the changes we'd made to his resume. I helped him recall the job applicants he'd wanted to hire. They'd had to interview with his boss and he'd instructed me to coach them.

That's right! Hiring managers coach their preferred applicants to fool their bosses into rubber-stamping the job offer.

Regardless of whether anyone wholeheartedly embraces the anything goes strategy, one thing is certain (more now during these difficult times than ever): if job applicants continue to play by the old rules as we have known them to date, it will likely prove as ruinous for them as it has for millions of others, resulting in extended joblessness, financial calamity, and loss of self-esteem.

For me, just like anyone else who has to work, it was about survival. And I say to all the naysayers who insist that nothing short of the truth is justified and who vehemently condemn anything but: it worked. As long as I stayed underground, my employment lasted for as long as I wanted it to. The one fact that no one can credibly dispute is that I never, ever helped a job applicant who wasn't qualified for the job based on the duties and responsibilities of the position. No one can credibly deny that I am good at my job—very good.

CHAPTER 11

Going Underground

Aldon's conscience took over, forcing him to hesitate. He couldn't accept the job without first confessing he hadn't been entirely truthful about some of his background. "I lied when I put a college degree on my resume," he said. "I never even went to college."

I cut him off when he tried to explain his reason for lying. "You need to stop talking," I said. "From this moment forward, you need to keep that information to yourself, and I'll do the same."

I pulled out a memo from the regional vice president of sales dated six weeks earlier and handed it to him. It read: "Aldon has it all. He is definitely qualified, and he knows the industry. However, I think I need someone younger for this team, so let's keep looking."

I took control of the conversation beginning with pointing out that there were all kinds of bad things going on at Kprints and provided details of actions by people like the vice president who had finally given the green light to hire him. Their actions were a lot worse than someone lying about a college degree, especially when the job didn't require a college degree in the first place.

I was in my fourth year with Kprints when Aldon and I came to that understanding. He was just the latest in a long list of applicants I'd coached although, he was one of the few I'd given details of the events during my early days at Kprints, which put me on this path of coaching and providing insider secrets to job applicants.

I confess, I'd planned to coach applicants even before I'd stepped across that Kprints threshold in October of 2000. I didn't know what I would find. What I did know was that the year I fought during my employment at FSfoods and the two years of litigation after had taken its toll.

Because of that struggle, I'd made myself a promise. If the situation at Kprints turned out to be like the one at FSfoods, the last thing I would do would be to speak up, complain, or challenge individuals or the system. I wasn't about to go along with discrimination, but I wasn't going to fight it out in the open either. Using the coaching tactics from my staffing company days was the only solution to ensure survival.

I broke the promise somewhere around the forty-fifth day. Incidentally, it was the same day my friendship with Meg began.

I encountered two competing versions of the Kprints culture within the first five weeks. Before my first encounter with the regional vice president of operations, everything I'd seen allowed me to believe that the culture of discrimination I'd experienced at FSfoods had been an aberration. There was no reason for me to have made any promise to myself in the first place. I wasn't under the illusion that the company would be utterly void of incidents of discrimination, as there will always be individuals who commit such acts. My only concern was whether or not it was company-wide. I was able to conclude that at Kprints, it wasn't.

The first two people to interview me for the position of district recruiter were female—one Hispanic, one white. The person who hired me, Julie, was the regional vice president of human resources and an African American female. I did not know Debra, the vice president of operations, before our meeting, but the fact that the position was held by a woman added to the image of a diverse and inclusive workforce. Hers was a position of power and authority traditionally held by men. It was notable that there were no minorities among the fifteen store managers who made up the Milwaukee district to which I was assigned. However, that was offset by the number of minorities and women I encountered at the regional office in Chicago.

I was forty-four years old and had worked for numerous companies by then and visited hundreds of others in my capacity as a headhunter. I'd never seen so many black people running around in a non-industrial setting. It was impressive and added to what I would later describe as my delusion, just as much as the promotion I received within the short time I was with the company.

They liked black people here and weren't afraid of them was the conclusion I came to when the regional recruiter position was offered. It was a leapfrog over the other recruiters, who all happened to be white and had years more time with the company. The promotion necessitated a meeting with Debra to discuss recruiting strategies for the operations and sales positions I would be responsible for.

"Don't say it. Stop. Don't say anything! I said *stop*!" That was me talking to myself before I told Debra, the regional vice president of operations that I wasn't going to discriminate against the job applicant she noticed sitting in the lobby. She told me the applicant was too old. I responded by saying, "We can't make a decision based on age. You know that. I'm not going to do it!"

Debra countered by asking about the candidate's experience. As I tried to give her details of his banking background, she cut me off. "Alright then, banking industry experience isn't applicable. He isn't qualified. Do you get it? Do you understand?"

Having already blown my plan, I had the urge to respond with something more. A resounding "Bullshit!" came to mind. The candidate had been referred by one of our recent hires who'd worked with him—in the banking industry. Hello! The only difference between them was the fact that the manager we hired was in his thirties. Of course, it would not have mattered what industry the banker had come from. She would have disqualified him using some other excuse—anything to make her point.

Three hours later, Julie of human resources voiced her disapproval with the way I'd handled myself with Debra. She also made it clear that age wasn't the only discrimination taking place. She told me the meeting with Debra was a test, and I had failed. Then she warned me about any future reluctance to go along with what Debra wanted. "Maybe I should have warned you," she said. "I thought with your background, you understood the game."

Then she went on to tell me how she had second thoughts about the promotion. How she didn't need a loose cannon that she would have to clean up after. And then the black thing came out. "Debra doesn't think a black person can recruit for her. She is afraid you are going to bring in a bunch of black people for management positions. In case you don't understand that you have a target on your back, I'm spelling it out for you right now."

By the time Julie finished with me I thought it best not to tell her about the conversation I'd had with the district sales manager for Chicago minutes before she'd cornered me. He was unhappy with the candidate I'd sent him to interview a few days earlier. He'd insisted that, in the future, I interview candidates in person before sending them to him. "The guy shows up in a wheelchair," he'd said. "That's what I'm talking about. You would have known that if you interviewed him in person. How is he going to get around to clients?"

His opinion about face-to-face interviews was as stupid as his question. "You saw his resume before I set up the interview," I'd told him. "You agreed to the interview because you saw the same thing I saw, that he has experience in outside sales, calling on customers. I confirmed that experience during the phone interview. Obviously, he was able to get around to customers with his last job, and he made it to the interview with you, so I'd say he really doesn't have a problem getting around. Besides," I added, "making a decision based on the wheelchair is against the law!"

This was my introduction to Kprints nine months before Jerry took over as CEO. It was the Kprints that would continue even as the rumor mill foretold of things to come. Word had it that during his first meeting with the board of directors, Jerry had said, "The first thing we need to do is get some color in this company, including in this room, because all I see is a bunch of old white guys." It was before I came to know the likes of Sean and Liz, who did what they could to ensure that diversity and inclusion meant more than just lip service.

By the time I met any of those people, I'd already given up on putting trust in the company's stated commitment to diversity, as well as the system in place that offered protection against retaliation. Debra and Julie spelled out reality in as clear terms as possible. I had no choice but to believe that they were more indicative of the culture than those first impressions, like "all the black people running around." Given that reality, I certainly wasn't about to trust anyone, regardless of how sincere they might have seemed.

Because here's the thing, and there's no way around this. I make this statement understanding that some people may judge that my internal mechanism has some missing pieces. Some people operate on the premise of hoping for the best while planning or expecting the worst; I only hope for and expect the best. I am challenged to consider the possibility of the worst. However, once I experience the worst, the pendulum swings to the other side of the scale. From that day forward, I expect the worst and act accordingly. The best is no longer possible.

I left the regional office that day damning myself for not sticking to my original plan. The ultimate goal was to keep the job by staying in good standing as a solid member of the go-along club. I was certain Julie's warning was the way of it and my days were numbered. Within a few days I'd gone from the image of the recruiting superstar whose performance warranted promotion in record time to "the wild card," someone Julie had to clean up after.

Dread was the emotion I felt as I made my way to conduct interviews at a store near the Wisconsin border, in Libertyville, Illinois. I dreaded the prospect of putting on a happy face for job applicants, dreaded the idea that I would do the bidding of people like Debra and Julie. I also dreaded the prospect of another job hunt.

By the time the Kprints sign came into view, I'd formulated a number of scenarios that allowed me to believe I could reconstitute the image of a "good black," willing to stay in his place. It might take some initial sucking up. I contemplated how I would do it. Maybe a comment to one of those people I had challenged earlier when they'd rejected a candidate because the person was too old or a minority. Maybe I would have a heart-to-heart with Julie, acknowledge the mistake and assure her I was on board. Anything to buy time, I told myself. Yes, I would have to look for another job, but at least it would be from a position of strength—being employed. In the meantime, I would, under that cover, coach job applicants as originally planned. I hadn't expected it to start that night, but it did, when I met Meg.

She was one of two candidates I interviewed that night. Fifty-something, just like the banker candidate vanquished by Debra, but she didn't look it. Her resume sported the kind of retail background that would make it difficult for Debra, or anyone following Debra's lead, to disqualify her. However, Meg advertised her age with the amount of experience she showed. The pretext they would be able to use to disqualify her without an open display of age-bias was hard to miss. Additionally, Meg had not worked in the past three years, and, in her last job, she'd held the position of regional director.

By looking at her resume, they could easily refuse to even interview her. They would say she was overqualified. They would also say she had been out of the workforce too long. I could certainly argue against that reasoning. I could point to the applicant they'd hired a week earlier who hadn't held a job for the past two years. There was also a case to be made against the overqualified excuse; there was the banker - I thought about throwing in Debra's face - the younger one who'd recommended the "old guy" - had held a similar regional position with the savings and loan he'd worked for. The alternative to arguing on her behalf and raising the ire of hiring managers who followed Debra's lead was to coach Meg and that's what I did.

"There are two ways we can do this," I said, after allowing Meg to walk me through her work history. "You have excellent background. It's the kind of top-grade experience the company looks for. I will highly recommend you whichever way you want to go. I can send your resume through as is, with my recommendation, or we can make some changes to eliminate any chance you'll be rejected before they have a chance to meet you.

"The first thing they are going to be concerned about is the fact that you haven't worked in three years," I told her. "The second, bigger problem is the fact that your experience is going to scare them. I can hear the district manager telling me that you're just taking this job to get something until the right one comes along."

I probably should have allowed her to get a word in at that point, but I wanted to get it all out, in case she was insulted by my suggestions. There had been times during my headhunting days when job applicants I'd tried to coach in a similar fashion looked at me as the bad guy with serious ethical issues.

"Like I said," I continued, "I can send your resume forward like this and you can take your chances, or we can make a few adjustments that will guarantee you'll get that face-to-face interview. My bet is you get the job."

Then I made some suggestions. We needed to fill in the last three years with a job at the store manager level. My reasoning was to show that she was employed and had already demonstrated that she could take as many as two steps down and remain at a company. The alternative would have been to eliminate the regional manager position altogether, but I didn't want her to lose that experience in case the next level position became available at Kprints.

"The last thing we need to do," I said, "is get rid of some of this old experience."

Then I said the worst of it—the reason for the coaching, the thing I shouldn't have said, although I tried to sugarcoat it.

"This is really a great company. I've been on board for a little over a month. It is a company you would be proud to work for. There is great opportunity. I was promoted after only thirty days on the job. But I'm sure you know there are all kinds of people at all companies, some who can't see past their own bias. And while I'm sure you can dazzle them and bust the stereotype when you interview, there's going to be some predisposition to discriminate because of your age."

Then I told her about the banker and the wheelchair guy. "But those people aren't indicative of Kprints," I insisted, meaning the managers who'd shown bias.

I was about to explain how I would be the one doing the background check and checking references so whatever we agreed to is what would be substantiated by me. But it wasn't necessary. She cut in with one word: "OK." In other words, shut up already. I get it.

Meg revised her resume that night. A week later Meg became a manager for Kprints. In less than six months, she was promoted to district manager.

The next day, I called that "old guy" who'd been rejected by Debra and told him why. Although nothing ever came of it, I offered to be a witness if he decided to file a discrimination complaint. I did the same with the wheelchair guy and took the extra step of providing both candidates with information on those who were hired instead of them.

The funny thing is Julie and Debra, the two people who set me on this path, didn't survive a restructure. It was as if I had never spoken up and shown my true colors—forgive the pun—during that visit to the regional office.

Without being the target of scrutiny, staying underground allowed me to remain employed at one company for more than six years. When I finally decided to leave, it was on my own terms.

After providing Aldon the details of my start at Kprints, he finally realized that he was no worse than anyone else. With that, he signed the offer letter.

Incidentally, a year or so later, when the senior vice president and general manager, Ander, decided to leave the company, he sent me an e-mail. In it, he praised the quality of management people I'd brought into the company and the significant contributions they'd made. Aldon was one of the people he was referring to in that statement.

CHAPTER 12

Chicken Chasers

I had no thoughts of going underground when I first came back to corporate America in 1996. Even if I wanted to coach job applicants, it would not have made any difference in the FSfoods environment.

The tactic of coaching a job applicant is based on the premise that there are established rules, standards, codes of conduct, demeanor, and attitude that I am able to pass on to the job applicant, thereby diminishing the opportunity for a hiring manager to weed the applicant out. FSfoods didn't have any consistent rules or standards that could be passed on. Until the day I threatened to go to the EEOC, I was forced to go along and hope that I could work within the system to affect change.

After two years of litigation, the evidence bore out that FSfoods retaliated against me because I opposed discriminatory hiring practices. They had to be faulted for allowing the hostile environment that existed at the time. They could have taken more immediate action, including making an example of some of those managers who'd discriminated by terminating them.

With the exception of those missteps and the decision to terminate my employment because I'd threatened to go to the EEOC, I cannot take away the fact that the company tried, in its own way, to change the culture of discrimination.

One of the significant policies they adopted was the establishment of a position profile. It was one thing to have a job description with preferred qualifications, as most companies do. It was another matter altogether to establish specific experience and related behavioral traits as criteria for determining a job applicant's suitability.

I sold this strategy under the guise that it established uniformity and consistency in hiring nationwide. Although that was true, it also provided an opportunity for me to challenge discriminatory decisions without getting in someone's face and coming off as the black guy they needed to fear. The profile I suggested, which was eventually adopted, was based on looking at past performance in relation to how long someone had stayed on the job, the difficulties of their previous job, and the environment.

The route sales job at FSfoods required long hours, often dawn to dusk. The job required knocking on doors, making deliveries, opening new accounts, getting dirty, lifting, hanging off the side of a truck—all on straight commission. These aspects of the job were included in the profile, effectively eliminating a hiring manager's ability to make decisions based on "anything goes."

Prior to implementing that profile, hiring was at the whim of a hiring manager. A division manager playing devil's advocate argued that the past performance criteria would eliminate that diamond-in-the-rough type of applicant. He told the story of the best salesperson he'd ever hired having no previous experience.

It had been in rural Missouri. The division manager had been riding with one of his drivers when they'd stopped at a farm. He'd noticed one of the farm workers rounding up chickens. He'd been amused by one of those clucks that refused to be corralled. He'd watched as the worker chased that chicken around the barnyard for several minutes before catching it. "He never gave up," the division manager said. "The bird had him running all over the place." The manager had never seen someone work so hard and with such hustle. He'd recruited him for a route sales position.

The division manager proposed to me that "chicken chasers" be part of the job profile if I wanted him to buy in.

Another manager in Denver made it clear that past experience didn't matter to him, that it all came down to that face-to-face interview. "He has to be on the edge of his chair," he said, "looking like he is ready to pop up and get going."

As the profile concept began to show results, the company sent me out in the field to conduct listening and consultation sessions with managers at all locations. As a part of that session, I presented the concept of past performance and behavior being the best predictor of future performance and behavior.

Establishing that profile was a monumental change for the company, and it worked. John, a longtime employee slated for a division manager slot, sent me a telex message: "You were right and now everyone knows. The only reason they don't have minorities and women down here is because they weren't hiring them, not because they don't apply, as they claimed. The profile eliminated all their excuses. I made them hire two African Americans and a woman."

I met my first African American management trainee in January of 2007, four months after the profile had gone into effect.

At a meeting in Memphis, the division manager who'd once claimed he couldn't hire blacks because they would get shot trying to deliver in the suburbs bragged about the two blacks he'd recently hired.

In May of that year, I received a fax message from a regional manager trainee indicating that all was well with the latest round of interviews. "The division manager was still reluctant, but I convinced him he had to hire the two women you sent. The profile forced him to admit his only reluctance was gender."

Despite the growing success of the profile process, there were two aspects of it the company refused to implement. They were nipped in the bud by the CEO himself. In January of 2007, I was asked to attend an executive staff meeting to discuss everything I was coming up against in the field. The idea was to have the regional VPs and other executives hear firsthand what I reported on a regular basis.

After the meeting, the CEO called me to his office and apologized for some of the comments I'd heard in the field and asked what he could do to make my job easier. I suggested that life would be a lot easier for the company if he initiated a policy that managers had to adopt the profile instead of it being voluntary. I also suggested they adopt a procedure where two higher level managers, maybe even a panel, had to review the rejection of a minority or female candidate. "It will go a long way toward ending the discrimination," I said.

I also suggested that with that kind of monitoring, negative comments like those I'd heard about minorities, women, "old guys," gays, or Jews would automatically dissipate. With that and the planned diversity and sensitivity training that was in the works, the company would have the cultural change everyone kept talking about, I explained.

As I spoke, I scribbled a flowchart of the process on a piece of paper and handed it to him. He looked at it for a second, then, as he responded, he balled it up and threw it in the trash. "I appreciate what you're saying," he told me, "but this business is based on strong local management control. Those managers live and die based on decisions they have to make to run their business. I'm not going to take hiring authority away from them."

Fast-forward to 2011 and a breaking news report: "Appeals Court Orders Company to Comply with EEOC Subpoena in Sex Bias Case." Apparently the EEOC launched a nationwide investigation of FSfoods for systemic discrimination.

Justia.com is a website that allows the public to search court dockets for pending litigation. Their records show over thirty discrimination-related cases against the company I'm calling FSfoods since 2009.

Since I left the company, some of these other less-publicized cases, which invariably led to the current deluge, have borne out the warnings and predictions I and others had made back in 1997.

In Southern California, a jury found that the company discriminated when making route assignments. The case involved a Hispanic route driver. In Missouri, the company settled a claim by two African American job applicants who claimed they were refused employment for the same reason as the Hispanic in California.

In 2010, I offered a similar warning and prediction to Liz and others in authority at Uniforms.

When Uniforms announced that a position profile was in the works for the territory sales position, I welcomed it with some measure of satisfaction. Was it possible that it was the result of my discrimination complaints? I'd reported incidents no less than seven times over the course of my employment. The most recent had been during that confidential meeting with the senior vice president of human resources and the corporate director of employee relations. They'd seemed attentive and genuinely shocked and concerned by the information. They'd taken notes when I'd warned that managers like Shitty were a ticking time bomb that would expose the entire culture.

If they were taking my discrimination complaint to heart, there was even the prospect that I could, at the very least, curtail coaching job applicants. That activity was a ticking time bomb as well, threatening to derail my discrimination case against the company. There is a precedent for cases being thrown out when, after the fact, it is determined an employee committed terminable offenses.

Age of job applicants was the issue for rejection managers most commonly stated verbally. Until the profile came out, the only way to combat the rejection of applicants, beyond my coaching, was to remind the manager that age discrimination was illegal and to argue the virtues of the concept of past performance and behavior as the truest predictor of future performance.

There were many negatives with the territory sales position. Uniforms experienced 50 to 70 percent turnover on an annual basis. The company offered low base pay, a complicated and limited commission structure, and strictly new business development, which meant no account management or regular customer base to go back to.

Given those parameters, if reducing turnover was a paramount goal, finding job applicants who demonstrated longevity in a similar situation was key. Ergo, the more experience the better.

Unfortunately, not only didn't the profile provide standards that would mitigate the opportunity to discriminate, it eliminated my ability to make the arguments I highlighted above.

In the following profile chart, I have emphasized the key requirements for the job of (Territory Sales Representative) in bold letters under the *External Hire Key Attributes* heading.

External Hire Key Attributes	Internal Promote Key Attributes	University/Jr College Hire Key Attributes
• <u>*Two to five years maximum outside/ new* sales acquisition experience</u> in a business to business company environment	• Proven track record of success in current role and total time with the company in achieving goals as well as strong interpersonal skills • Service department	• Has held a job while going to school • Has demonstrated leadership in sports or activities • Satisfactory academic performance

The last thing I expected was a criterion limiting the number of years of experience. But there it was, two to five years maximum.

The profile gave a manager, courtesy of the company, license to discriminate based on age. The arguments I used in an attempt to thwart it became moot. From that day forward, all any manager needed to do was refer to the profile when they rejected an applicant, whether their true motivation was to feed their bias against older workers or not.

CHAPTER 13

The Wild West

Darren walked away after turning in the integrity and honesty pre-employment assessment. Before the store door closed behind him, I called him back. I handed him a new test, told him why he needed to take it again, and gave him the correct answers to questions 14, 23, and 42. He'd answered question 23 correctly the first time, but not the other two. All three were automatic elimination questions, if they were answered incorrectly despite the fact that we were instructed to tell job applicants there were none. The test introduction matched the general statement we made: the assessment would not be a determining factor when making the hiring decision.

That was 1979. I was twenty-three-years-old and a store manager for a privately-held clothing chain. Integrity and honesty assessments had taken the place of lie detectors. It was the first time I felt the need to coach a job applicant about anything. It was also my first taste of assessments. The experience soured me on their validity and necessity, for a variety of reasons. In that situation, the first problem was that the company expected us to lie to the applicant. Second, the test instructions lied. Yet, the job applicant was expected to tell the truth? Please! On top of that, if the applicant told the truth, as Darren did—that he'd tried marijuana, swiped a quarter from his mother's purse when he was a child, and was hesitant about turning anyone else in if he knew they were being dishonest—automatically disqualified him.

I couldn't live with that. I told job applicants like Darren the truth about how we used the test and gave them the answers. I left it to them to decide for themselves how to answer the questions. I didn't want them to take that test without knowing that their answers affected the employment decision.

Those were the grand old days. Since then, assessments have evolved in sophistication and administration. The way an assessment is used affects every job applicant, regardless of age, race, or gender. Over the years, these tests have proliferated in corporate America and cover every aspect—skills, personality, integrity, morals, you name it.

In addition to the evidence that many of these tests are culturally biased, very often the results trump actual experience, which may actually contradict the results. When used for people who have verifiable, quantifiable experience, the tests are a waste of time and money. When a decision is made to disqualify an applicant solely based on the results of an assessment and that applicant's experience contradicts the finding from the assessment, it's nothing less than idiocy.

The one area where assessments might make sense is when you are dealing with a candidate who has no experience in a field or job. However, even in that case, I would argue they are unreliable because, despite claims to the contrary, these assessments can be and are manipulated by the assesse and the assessor.

The opportunity for a front-line manager to change the outcome of a test is virtually nonexistent. During the past thirty-two years, there have been two other times when that opportunity presented itself. The first time was in 1993. My staffing company had a contract with a Southern-based restaurant chain. The deal was $2,300 for every general manager hired. They needed one hundred five of them. It was one of those volume-deal exclusives that I'd dreamed of. I thought we were in the money when the first fifteen candidates were advanced to second and third interviews in the first month. However, by the end of forty-five days, every one of those first fifteen—and another twelve—was rejected. The company hired a total of three people through our company.

The applicants had been knocked out of consideration because of answers they'd given on the assessment test. Time and money for three recruiters to work the volume account, not to mention advertising expense, far exceeded the piddly $6,900 in fees we collected. I was ready to cancel the deal when one of my recruiters with contacts at the company made a phone call and then rushed out the door. Three hours later, he returned with a copy of the assessment questions and answers. There were eight knockout questions. All future candidates received those answers.

In 2010, Uniforms' vice president of sales, John, had a plan. Initially, I was shaking my head when the company introduced a new pre-employment assessment for sales applicants. However, there was one positive. John established a threshold score for determining the viability of an applicant. It meant several things to me. First, I finally had a standard that would be used uniformly throughout the company. Second, I was able to use the standard to argue against any decision by a manager to refuse to interview or hire a protected-class applicant. Overall, making this move created an opportunity for me to work within the system.

John set a minimum score for one of the measurements, competitive drive, at 80 percent. It applied to every applicant, regardless of what they looked like. From a recruiting standpoint, that criterion, along with the other specific scoring mechanism, was almost as good as a position profile. By establishing criteria or scores in different areas, a manager now had difficulty qualifying or disqualifying job applicants on a whim or discriminatory bias.

It eliminated the kind of idiocy like that demonstrated by a couple of managers in Florida. The district sales manager there told the HR representative that he judged job applicants based on whether they had scuff marks on the bottom of their shoes. Another manager made his decision based on whether the applicant was someone he would feel comfortable bringing home to dinner. This harkened back to the stupidity of the division manager at FSfoods in 1996 who'd said, "I only hire people who are members of my church or who were referred by someone from my church." It didn't matter what an applicant's experience was.

THE WILD WEST

John had some qualities that were rare at Uniforms. He was a top-grade. He operated efficiently when making hiring decisions. It was about job applicants demonstrating experience and qualifications—period. When he was terminated as part of a downsizing, I predicted the negative consequences. What I didn't know was how quickly the strategy of maintaining strict qualifications through his assessment standards would fall.

The company thought nothing of relegating his duties to two individuals who were considerably less qualified. One of those individuals I've mentioned a few times, Adam. He was incompetent, and he discriminated based on age and race. With his new responsibilities, he had the influence to advance his philosophy and strategy to a larger group of managers. Before John was gone, the standards were reduced. It was back to every manager for himself or herself. It was back to what I call the wild, wild West (every person for themselves, shooting from the hip with whatever reason they wanted to come up with to determine whether a job candidate was suitable).

Although the official criterion for the assessment was reduced to a 50 percent threshold for competitive drive, it fluctuated over time. Individual managers, regardless of the official number, either refused to interview an applicant unless the individual met a threshold they agreed with or hired them even if the competitive drive number didn't meet the standard. In one instance, a director of sales bragged that a candidate he'd hired had turned into a top performer within weeks of getting a territory, despite the fact that his competitive drive score was less than 10 percent. He was equally proud of the fact that the seller had little previous sales experience. Even I would have disqualified the job applicant with no sales and a score that low.

My point is this: there was no consistent standard, and on that basis a manager could and did reject or hire a job applicant on nothing more than his or her own whim.

The structure of the test made it impossible for me to coach applicants on how to answers the questions in a way that would make the scores come out favorably. However, the administration of the results went through the recruiter who set up the online assessment for the applicant. So when the scores came back to me, I changed them before forwarding the test to the hiring manager. I changed the score any time a job applicant had quantifiable experience that contradicted a score that said they couldn't be an outside sales rep for the company. I also confess to changing scores for individuals who may not have had that verifiable experience. If a manager showed a pattern of rejecting a protected-class individual, I changed the applicant's scores to get them that interview—just because.

CHAPTER 14

Got Me

On January 11, 2011, the Equal Employment Opportunity Commission announced that a record number of employment discrimination complaints were filed with the agency in fiscal year 2010.

As a result of investigations, mediations, pretrial settlements and litigation, the agency obtained $404 million for victims of discrimination—the highest amount ever. The EEOC also announced that, for the first time, the number of complaints filed for discriminatory retaliation surpassed the number filed for race discrimination.

Adverse actions can come in many shapes and sizes. In addition to false performance appraisals and discipline and discharge of the complaining employee, many actions that put the complainant in a more unfriendly working environment are considered retaliatory—actions like moving the person from a spacious, brightly lit office to a dingy closet, depriving the person of previously available support services (like administrative help or desktop computer), or cutting off challenging assignments.

The law deliberately does not take a laundry list approach when considering a retaliation case because, according to the Seventh Circuit Court of Appeals, "unfortunately, its forms are as varied as the human imagination will permit."

At Uniforms, the final push of retaliatory action began in March of 2011. Company executives took over where Shitty left off. It was a little over a year after I'd called out the company's discriminatory culture and nine months after I'd filed an EEOC complaint. That's how long it took them to figure out how to deal with someone who, by their own account, was a top performer.

Their strategy began with the midyear performance review. During the nine months prior, the company had responded to my EEOC complaint by offering, among other things, praise for my work, along with proof. It was their claim that the decision to move me from the North to a larger region in the Midwest was due to their confidence and satisfaction with my performance. That statement was their official response to a government agency in October, less than two months before the end of the six-month period on which the midyear performance appraisal was based.

They handed me a gift when the midyear appraisal listed fourteen performance issues covering everything from communication problems and unauthorized use of recruiting resources to lack of initiative, refusal to offer assistance and suggestions on recruiting alternatives, and failure to achieve recruiting goals.

Most workers have gone through the appraisal process and therefore know that the measurements are pre-established before the beginning of the appraisal period. That's how everyone knows what duties and goals are to be met and considered at appraisal time. In an attempt to justify the performance issues noted, the company changed the predetermined criteria originally established and added additional items. However, even with those changes they had to manufacture incidents and events in order to justify what was written.

The problem for them—and this goes back to my comment earlier about assholes having the additional trait of being arrogant and stupid—was that they didn't consider or overlooked the possibility that I had documentation which disproved every negative thing they included in the performance appraisal.

One of the issues they raised: "We observed your reluctance to try other recruiting alternatives and ideas, e.g., job fairs, etc. Often your only suggestion is Monster.com, which, as you know, is not a company-supported alternative."

In writing and verbally, they accused me of poor customer service directly related to this situation, and they said, "This does not exhibit the level of accountability to drive and deliver the results that is expected."

Now, here's an e-mail I received from a general manager during the period in question:

07/15/2010 11:02 AM ct

To: Brian D NordUNIFORMS@UNIFORMS

From: Ralph P

Cc:

Subject: Re: heads-up

Brian,

Thanks for the heads-up. I also appreciate the direction on the career fair. Traci, Lisa, and I will all be in attendance. We also found another one 2 days later that we will be attending. We're hopeful that between the 2 fairs we find the rep to fill the open territory in WPB as well as our 2 bench positions in Fort Lauderdale.

Thanks for all of your support. You've done an awesome job for the Fort Lauderdale Production Company thus far. The 4 hires you recently provided me have all sold significant amounts of business early on:

Eddie B.—8 accounts sold so far!

Margaret L.—Closed a $600/wk account last week.

Mark V.—2 accounts sold.

Edwardo P.—Closed $300 account this week.

Just thought you would appreciate seeing how your efforts are impacting business results. Thanks again for all you do!

And here's a comment from my performance review in June of 2010, part of my instructions related to performance expectations for the new appraisal period:

"Thank you for your feedback on Zoominfo.com and the 'blind postings' through Monster. I want you to continue to share these best practices with the group so we can continue to improve the recruiting brand."

As you can read, both of these documents contradict the false claims made in the appraisal, that use of Monster.com was unauthorized and that I didn't suggest job fairs. These are just two of more than seventy such documents.

Additional proof materialized a month after I was forced out. I received a phone call from one of the HR representatives with whom I'd shared the content of my mid-year review. She said, "You're not going to believe this one. I couldn't wait for the conference call to end so I could call to tell you. Guess which job posting service the company is going with—exclusively. Monster.com! Can you believe that, after the crap they gave you?"

Although I officially disputed the false performance appraisal, I welcomed it for the benefit of evidence to prove I was, in fact, retaliated against because of my opposition to discrimination.

If that had been the end of the company's shenanigans, I would have probably stayed with them a while longer, even though, as a matter of conscience, it became increasingly difficult for me to recruit applicants into what I knew was a horrible culture for anyone.

The legal term is "constructive discharge." Constructive discharge occurs when an employee is forced to quit because the employer has made working conditions unbearable. Unbearable conditions include discrimination or harassment or receiving a negative change in pay or work for reasons that are not work-related.

This was the point where Uniforms was able to register a temporary win. They were already putting the screws to me leading up to the performance review. I went from having one supervisor to two. They double-teamed me with micro-management, criticism, and questions about everything I did. This was despite the fact that my two regions were the only regions out of the company's five, that were meeting or exceeding the 100 percent recruiting goal.

The company insisted that I track every job applicant on a separate spreadsheet, even though the company used an online system that automatically tracked and reported on activity. Previously, I'd worked directly with managers and had the autonomy and authority to advance recruiting initiatives and strategies in conjunction with their requests. Suddenly, I had to get approval. Managers refused to speak with me one-on-one. Any time there was a conversation, both my supervisors had to be on the line.

While the company was increasing expectations, they were also supporting attempts to eliminate me from the same recruiting assignments they were holding me accountable for. Although they would make the claim in my performance review that I didn't communicate with managers, one of them specifically forbade me to speak with a GM who had a recruiting problem. I was told to use an outside recruiter and was then criticized for doing so.

The effect was growing, uncontrollable anger. The problem with anger is that it leads to situations like when I yelled and hung up on Liz. And when it came to these two HR Directors, there were a number of moments when I used insulting words—like "idiocy," "incompetence," and "stupid"—to describe them and their actions. I was just stating fact; however, it would have been an easy call for them to claim insubordination.

Then, due to my verbal objections and resistance, I received a written document, which, among other things, included this line: "You will be held accountable for 100 percent fill of all positions 100 percent of the time at each individual location regardless of whether you are directly involved in the recruiting or not."

Beyond being responsible for every position regardless of whether I was the one doing the recruiting or had any control, they'd changed a more significant parameter. During the prior two years, the measurement of 100 percent had been based on a region as a whole. One location might be down one sales position, but another location might be up two or three. The total for the region made up the 100 percent. Now, every location had to be at or above 100 percent, and I was responsible even though I may not have been the one doing the recruiting.

These new, impossible standards became more proof for my retaliation complaint. In their stupidity, the company made the mistake of not applying these same standards to the other regional recruiting manager. She received her review weeks before I did. There were no changes to her job. There were no changes in standards, and, despite the fact that her regions were well below mine in recruiting performance, she received no negatives on her review.

That was it for me. I resigned on April 4, 2011. However, as of this writing, the battle continues with a pending hearing to determine probable cause. It won't be over until a jury in a federal courtroom hears all the evidence. My goal is nothing less than a full-scale federal investigation of the company and the kind of legal determination that will force them to follow the law.

CHAPTER 15

Student Rights

Without knowing anything else, a glimpse of the acts of defiance during my childhood years would allow anyone to predict that I would always have an aversion to acts of abuse of authority or power.

The last beating I remember occurred around my eleventh birthday. Dad was working second shift at the battery plant. Mom had some social event. My brothers and I had been instructed to limit our activities to studying in our rooms or watching TV in the family room.

It wasn't long after Mom's car turned out of the driveway that I came up with the brilliant idea of cleaning the house. We were still at it when Mom came home a few hours later. It was right around the time Dad made his nightly check-in phone call. She described what everyone was doing and then put the phone to my ear and told me to tell my Dad what I was up to. She had to hold the phone for me because my hands were deep in dishwater. "I'm doing the dishes," I said.

As she pulled the phone back, Mom asked, "Is that what I told you to do?"

"No, ma'am," I said. "We just wanted to surprise you."

Her tone was pleasant as she continued the conversation with Dad. I remember some of the conversation. She explained that when she left the house, we were sitting in front of the TV. "I come home and find all this going on," she said.

When she hung up the phone, she made me stop what I was doing and then turned to the oldest, Bob. It was his fault we went against her instructions, and she went on about all the bad things that might have happened.

Two days later, Saturday morning, and the belt came out. My brother Randal and I shared the room closest to my parents, so we got it first. Then Dad went across the hall to Bob and Ron. From the screams, I could tell Ron got it the first of those two. Bob took a whack and then yelled out that he'd tried to stop us from cleaning. "It was Brian's idea!" he yelled. "I told them not to do it. But they went ahead anyway."

"He gets it twice then," I heard my dad say. Bob was spared additional stings from the belt as Dad turned back toward my room.

Given the history of violent punishment for something as innocent as what occurred during that incident, even I have to wonder what possessed me to risk that kind of wrath by getting involved in a protest the following fall when I entered the seventh grade.

STUDENT RIGHTS

For years, I wondered why I didn't get a beating after my Dad had to interrupt needed sleep to get me from school. Sometime in my twenties he explained it like this: that summer he came to a decision that it was time to stop using a belt and start talking. That was it. The beatings were part of their parenting plan all along. It had been the way their parents had done it, so it had made sense to them. But Dad thought it had gone too far the last time. He was thankful for the opportunity to back off Bob, whom he already knew was too old for anything to come from the pain.

As we drove home that morning, after Dad had had to listen to the vice principal scold him for my conduct, there was only talk. The general theme was I had to follow the rules, whatever they were.

The protest that had sent me to the principal's office was in response to a hastily established dress code that insisted that all button-down shirts with tails had to be tucked in. Among other disparities, the rules weren't applied to girls.

I was sent to the principal's office when I refused to comply with a teacher's demand that I tuck my shirt in. Instead, I cited the rules from the school board handbook governing dress code. It clearly demonstrated that the John Burroughs Junior High administration had deviated from the policy when they'd instituted their dress code standard. It said something like only school board-established dress codes shall be instituted. And the dress code established by the school board said nothing about shirttails—in or out. I won that battle at school, but at home the ultimatum was "tuck in your shirt or we go out and by shirts without tails."

I got into trouble again a year later as the vice president of student council when I took the words of future

Wisconsin governor Lee Dreyfus to heart. He was the chancellor of a college and the keynote speaker at our retreat for student council members. In that speech, he echoed King's message of civil disobedience and challenged us all to exercise our rights as students. I was picked to deliver a speech/report about our trip and plans for the school to the student body. When our teacher advisor read the speech, he censored it, pointing out that the charter of the student council gave veto power to school administrators. The system, as I saw it, was rigged. Exercising student rights was out, and talking about them was definitely out.

I gave the speech anyway. Two days of detention and my parents were summoned to school. Despite being a good student, despite participation in the student council, despite being a jock with MVP honors for competition in intramural basketball, track, and football, school administrators branded me a troublemaker and couldn't wait until that day came when I had to move on to high school.

The permanent break from my parents' way of thinking came my first year in high school. The swim coach ran his class as if he were still in the Marine Corps. Even to this day, I can picture the barrel-hard chest as he stood there in a Superman pose, without the cape. The message was clear—you don't want to mess with me. As soon as we were lined up along the bleachers overlooking the pool, he sounded off the rules. Number one: if your hair doesn't look like this—he pointed to his crew cut—or like that—he pointed to the only other black kid in the class, Jerome Bishop, whose hair was cut close to the scalp—you need to wear a swim cap. "Cut it or wear a cap!" he yelled. Cutting off any further discussion, he blew his whistle, which was the signal for us to get in the pool.

His reasoning was that long hair tends to have more fallout and it clogs the pool filter and drain. I protested—at first, by sitting out swim class. By the third time, he insisted I participate and handed me a swim cap to cover my huge Afro. That's when I finally spoke up. It was discriminatory to treat those of us with long hair differently. "Besides," I said, "when my hair gets wet, it shrinks, so it will look like Jerome's."

That wasn't good enough. It was his way or the office. I headed for the office. When word of my latest brush with authority reached home, Dad put it to me like this: "You either wear the cap, or I'll cut your hair myself and it will look just like mine." Dad's hair was cut to the scalp. I decided to get a trim, which reduced the size of my Afro significantly. I sure as hell wasn't going to wear some sissy swim cap.

The next day, I went to the swim coach, first to apologize as my parents had demanded, and then for his approval of the newly trimmed me. He looked me up and down and gave me an "I guess I can live with that, but it could be a little shorter."

OK, now here's where I went too far, and, to be honest, I can't tell you why. Maybe it was just ego—he had won and yet he was still kind of rubbing my nose in it. So I said, "You're really ignorant, you know that?" Then I walked away. Three days detention. My parents had to come to school and a threat was made that I would be sent to one of those schools for troublemakers and hard cases.

This time around there were no choices. As punishment, Dad commanded, "You are going to participate in every class and you are going to wear a swim cap." That was it—case closed. Well, sort of. The gym locker areas were centrally located with adjacent doors that led to the pool on one side and the football field on the other. When players came in from the field after a day's practice, the dirt from their cleats mixed with the water that dripped from our time in the pool, creating a dirty mix.

I used the unsanitary condition as a reason why I wouldn't participate in swim. I wasn't going to walk barefoot through that dirty water to go back and forth from the pool. Not to mention the fact that you were standing in that same dirty mess (it really wasn't that bad) after getting out of the shower. The coach, to his credit, tried to reason with the hard case and gave me one more chance to fall in line. I had until the next swim class. He expected me to be ready to go. I had two days. I used it to contact the school board and file a complaint over the dirty conditions.

I won that battle—but not the way I wanted. Participation in swim was cancelled for everybody for a week until they figured out what to do. The solution: sandals were supplied to everyone. I spent the rest of the summer wearing that stupid swim cap.

My point of these digressions into the rebellious incidents of my youth is to drive home not only the point that I possessed an automatic reflex to do something about injustice, but also that, although resistance to any form of injustice was awakened in me at a young age, that which I describe was the worst of it. As much as I knew that consequences had the potential to be dire, these situations were nothing compared to what the majority of African Americans dealt with.

I experienced those injustices as an American, not because I am African American. Despite the fact that the majority of African Americans had a difficult existence, my life was good and my prospects seemed limitless. I have always been able to live where I wanted to live, in the suburbs, despite the fact that even after all these years few other minorities ever seem to materialize. I enjoyed the rewards of advancement in corporate America. When I ventured out to run my own business, I was able to get a loan and grow the business. I succeeded and failed on my own.

Even my marriage to an Irish/German, red-headed beauty from the white enclave of the south side barely caused a ripple. That is saying something, considering it was 1980 in Milwaukee, Wisconsin. Even today, it's one of the most segregated communities in the United States. If there was a voice of decent, it had nothing to do with race. There was legitimate shock at how quickly my wife and I had come together. Three days after our first date, we decided to get married. Bam! No one thought it would last three years, let alone the thirty we have been together.

I did not have the typical life of an African American; the color of my skin and my heritage was of little to no consequence until I entered corporate America. It has been in my professional life as a recruiter that the same injustice against others—the kind that I seldom experienced myself until my attempts to call out those injustices —is what stirs my conscience for civil disobedience in very much the same way it did when I was child. Back then, I was immune, thanks to my parents' creating an environment void of racial strife. My status in corporate America also made me immune from those injustices—as long as I was willing to go along with the status quo.

This brings me back to that quote from Martin Luther King Jr. Failure in my attempts to openly change the corrupt and inherently discriminatory hiring process calls for civil disobedience. It is the basis of that quote—the idea that "non-cooperation with evil is as much a moral obligation as is cooperation with good" —that, for me, suggests that not only is it OK to coach and guide job applicants through a corrupt system that seeks to eliminate them in violation of law and all reason, it's a moral obligation. It's equally justifiable for a job applicant to protect himself or herself by not following the rules that have been set up to eliminate them.

Some theories hold that civil disobedience is only justified against governmental entities. However, there is also the argument that disobedience in opposition to the decisions and policies of nongovernmental entities is equally justified.

CHAPTER 16

Regrets

Bob Firtts barely made it out of the small Georgia town alive.

He moved his wife and family to Orlando, Florida, to escape a situation that is best described as a plot similar to that of John Grisham's novel *The Firm*. In the film based on the book, Tom Cruise played a young attorney forced to work undercover by federal authorities seeking to expose the control of a prestigious Tennessee law firm by organized crime.

Instead of a lawyer, Bob was a banker. He went to the FBI instead of them coming to him. He exposed the financial institution's control by organized crime. Anyway, that's how he told it. He offered the information to explain his reluctance and frustration at winding up in Orlando. After six months searching for a job, he was beginning to take to heart what he was hearing from the few acquaintances he'd developed since arriving. His resume generated phone interviews; however, the phone conversation with a prospective employer never led to the next step of in-person interview. One banking executive confirmed what others had told him. His deep Southern drawl might have played well in northern Florida, with so many people crossing that Georgia-Florida line. However, in central and southern Florida it was a different story. The prevailing stereotype that a Southern accent also meant "hick" or dim-witted and slow in both thought process and physical movement spelled difficulties for Bob. The executive told him, "Unless you do something about your speech, you're going to continue to have a hard time."

It was late 1990. If not for the fact that Grisham's book didn't go to print until 1991, I could swear Bob adopted the story in order to garner some sympathy or cover up the true reasons for his life-changing move to Florida. In fact, when the movie came out years later, that is what I thought, until I did some research and determined Bob's ordeal preceded the book. At the time however, I was shaking my head in disbelief that I had, despite skepticism, given him the benefit of the doubt. As a headhunter and company owner, my propensity to trust people at face value had almost ruined my business several times prior.

Here are a few examples. Part of my business focused on career counseling, including writing resumes and business proposals. There was this guy who sucked me into believing that he was the heir to the Hess oil fortune. His name wasn't

Hess, however the longer name he used included Hess. He produced official-looking documents from corporate giants like Disney and Hess as proof that he was involved in major marketing development deals. His investments were broad, and he considered my business consulting services a great opportunity that he was willing to invest in. This went on for weeks as he paid me to write and rewrite a marketing proposal for Disney. I questioned why Disney, with its millions and formidable marketing expertise, needed someone like him. His answer made sense; large corporations used outside contractors all the time. Maybe I was stupid, but there was no reason not to believe him. He wasn't getting anything from me that he didn't pay for. The thousands of dollars in fees were paid in cash.

The overall image he portrayed with the money, expensive car, tailored suits, matching silk shirts and ties, and Rolex watch helped advance his claim that he was attached to wealth and had high-powered contacts. His offer to include me in a meeting he had scheduled with none other than corporate golden boy Michael Eisner was the final hook, making me a believer. So much so that I went out and bought a new suit for the occasion; I spent $1200 dollars before I was done. Although I was hard-pressed to understand exactly what he might be scamming me for, my skepticism began to rise when the meeting was first postponed and then cancelled altogether. When I couldn't find the luxury office space he had designated for our new joint venture, I made a call to Hess headquarters in New York. There was only one heir to the Hess fortune, and he worked at Hess in New York.

A year before that, I'd been in negotiations with another client who'd frequented my office for business proposal services as well. He'd wanted to partner with me to expand my services throughout the region. He'd received my services six times within a two-week period before his first check bounced. A few months after I'd ended my relationship with him, he was indicted for fraud. Apparently, using the same scheme he'd been running on me, he'd talked a local restaurateur into partnering with him to market her special barbecue sauce. In her case, he'd conned her out of $100,000.

Bob was in my office for help. He was running out of money and options. As a transplant from the Midwest myself, I didn't see much difference between the way Bob and people born and raised in central Florida spoke. After four years of dealing with employers, a slow Southern drawl was a positive attribute when compared to the resistance I received when I presented job applicants from the North. That heavy New York or Massachusetts accent induced a lot of comments condemning the job applicant as "nothing but a snowbird." The terminology, traditionally used to describe a person who vacations in or moves to a warmer climate during cold weather, was attached negatively to anyone beyond the Southern states. The inference was they were like vacationers. They expected sun and fun and not to work too hard.

This attitude of disqualifying someone simply because they weren't local was one of the reasons I advised applicants to eliminate states and other locations on their resume. In some cases, we advised them to include information that indicated they traveled to or worked in the Florida market for a number of years before moving there. Anything to meet the standard criterion that a job applicant needed to prove they were going to stick once they experienced the heat and came to grips with the reality that working in Florida wasn't all sun and fun or that the rules of hard work don't apply.

Applicants who took our advice advanced to face-to-face interviews. Unfortunately, some of them were still rejected for the job because of their Northeastern accents. That's what client companies told us. But not once in four years had I heard of a job applicant being denied a position because of a Southern accent.

By the time our meeting ended, Bob accepted my offer of a job as a recruiter/counselor. It just so happened that I wanted to advance the financial division of my staffing company and needed someone who knew the ins and outs of the industry.

My proposal offered a paycheck without any concern of a long-term commitment on his part. It was an opportunity for him to gain contacts and information on jobs that were more to his liking and professional background while earning a salary and helping me to grow my business.

The relationship worked as planned for both of us. My financial services accounts grew quickly and Bob landed a job as a branch manager for a regional savings and loan. During his final days, he reminisced about all the assholes he'd come in contact with. "This has been an eye-opening experience, one I'll never forget," he said. "What I still can't believe is the number of employers who insisted they wouldn't hire blacks." And he found it incredible that women were routinely dismissed based on stereotypes that he had not been accustomed to hearing in his professional life. On a number of occasions, he told the story of the title company manager who'd been only interested in hiring "a nice-looking white girl who I can sit and look at all day."

Until the manager had made the call to us, he'd been working with the state employment commission to keep from paying a fee. "All they send me is fat people and bohemian-looking black people," he'd said.

Bob admitted there were times when he'd gone with the status quo during his Georgia days, explaining that there had been no blacks at any of the banks he'd managed because "that's just the way it was." He always pressed the point that it wasn't him personally. He saw images of himself in that title company manager, who was also a transplant from Georgia. "Never again," Bob said. "Now I know."

I'd experienced this "reborn" type of awakening in others before. People who'd discriminated suddenly changed their ways after experiencing the discrimination themselves. I welcomed it, especially in Bob's case. The relationship that led to the branch manager job for him also resulted in a contract with my staffing company to supply manager trainee candidates. With Bob as my primary contact, I pictured dollar signs.

I also experienced how quickly people like Bob, once they have reestablished their place in the corporate structure, revert to their old ways. So it wasn't a surprise when he called me to reject Than Nyugen as an applicant.

In his deep Southern drawl, Bob asked. "Does he even speak good English? What is he anyway, Vietnamese? A big part of this job is customer service—you know, answering incoming calls. I can't have someone who speaks broken English, like they just got off the boat."

Bob had yet to hear Than speak. He'd made these assumptions based strictly on seeing a resume. After I explained American-born Than's history, including how he spoke—like a white guy—I emphasized how he was a perfect match to the job. "You want trainees with a major in finance. He's got that. You asked for trainees who'd worked while they were in college. He did that. He has a 3.8 grade point average!"

It wasn't enough. "Yeah, Brian," he said. "But you know, I still have to say no because, you know, I just can't picture someone answering the phone saying, 'Hi, my name's Than.' First response out of their mouths is gonna be, 'What? Than?' They'll spend the first few minutes just trying to get his name right!"

That's when I changed Than's name. "I'll fax over the resume he gave me before we changed it," I told Bob. "You'll see he goes by the nickname Don. I told him he needed to use his formal name on the resume . He's American-born. He speaks better English than you or me." Then I pointed to the retail work Don had done while working his way through school. "All these years he's been working with customers on the phone and in person at the same business. If it worked for them, it will work for you."

It was the first time I lied for a job applicant without them knowing beforehand. It was the first time I had to explain to a job applicant, in detail, why I lied and went so far as to change his name.

Reluctantly, Bob agreed to the interview. When Than didn't get the job, it was the first time I agreed to be a witness in a discrimination complaint. My last-ditch effort to get Don the job also ended my relationship with Bob and the financial service company; I made Bob aware that I'd offered to help Than with a discrimination complaint.

When I think of those staffing company days, I am torn by emotions of guilt and pride. Pride because, despite the hundreds of managers we did business with who discriminated, I never wavered in my optimism that, by and large, the companies themselves weren't discriminatory. The guilt comes from realizing that I was naïve about that.

Until 1994, I stuck with the idea of giving companies the benefit of the doubt and only coaching job applicants to withhold and change information if I knew for a fact that the company or the person we were dealing with wasn't on the up and up. My faith, or, rather, my refusal to face the evidence of a generally corrupt environment that nurtured and sustained discrimination and unfair treatment of job applicants, hurt people.

As an employment counselor, I was accustomed to telling people before sending them for an interview not to worry about how old they were or looked—it was about how they handled themselves. I told them that even if there was a predisposition to reject someone because of his or her age, it was usually based on a stereotype. Once the decision maker had a chance to see that the candidate didn't fit the stereotype, a decision based on qualifications was soon to come.

My advice was the same for women, minorities, and those with disabilities. It was my gospel, and I believed every word. I believed it because I thought I was living proof that everything I said was true. I would even point to my own success as an example to make sure they got the picture.

For every job applicant my staff and I advised to lie and withhold information based on knowledge of a company's prior hiring practices, there were just as many who received our standard "be honest and up front" advice.

Most of our advice was centered around getting applicants to understand the negatives they might face in the job market and helping them put together presentations that highlighted skills the employer was looking for. We'd advise applicants how to explain gaps in employment instead of eliminating them and how to answer interview questions, and we counseled them on where their experience would be best utilized in relation to the types of jobs that were available.

It was the kind of corporate-friendly advice that left them open to elimination for legitimate reasons as well as illegal ones. However, the unfairness that I came to grips with during the last two years of my staffing company days—the fact that the legitimate and illegal reasons that companies used were applied unequally— moved me to offer the same coaching to all job applicants who walked through our doors, whether they needed it or not.

I can't tell you the exact day I made this decision, but I do remember it started with a recovering cancer patient. He was a white male in his mid-thirties and a single parent. Until the cancer ravaged his body, he'd been a highly paid engineer for a defense contractor. When I met him, he had been out of work for over a year. His cancer was in remission. He was desperate to get back to work, but his prospects dried up as soon as he divulged the cancer history. He'd been working with another recruiting company that had told him he had to divulge the cancer, even though the company knew he wouldn't get a second look from an employer. I didn't know if any of that was true. My advice to him was to test the theory, and he agreed; there would be no more disclosures about his medical history. He was healthy now, and that's all that mattered. Because of his extraordinary background, he received a job offer within thirty days, one that included full relocation expenses to another state.

From that day forward, every job applicant who walked through our doors received the full measure of everything we believed and understood about the job market. How they chose to proceed was up to them; however, we left no scenario off the table. At the least, it was our responsibility to school them based on the information we had, whether they wanted to know it or not.

I regret all the times people passed through our doors and went on their merry way on my advice and faith in an idea of how things were supposed to be instead of the way they were.

Today, as I write this, reflecting on the number of people who didn't get the benefit of the whole of our knowledge, I am at loss to explain how it was that I went back to corporate America and, for a time, blindly followed and espoused the same faith.

CHAPTER 17

Culture

Jim Adamson knew going in as CEO of Advantica Corporation, the parent company of Denny's Restaurants (previously named Flagstar), that systemic discrimination against minorities and women existed. National headlines had reported incidents of discrimination that led to EEOC investigations of the company.

"Our Worst Hour." That's how Adamson titles the first chapter of his book *The Denny's Story*. In the book, he describes the incidents of discrimination and racism that led to the firestorm of negative publicity, related protests, EEOC investigations, and a multimillion-dollar settlement.

Although the focus of the lawsuits involved Denny's discriminatory treatment of minority customers, there was also a case to be made that the discrimination extended to employment, and Jim Adamson addressed it head-on.

Reporter Anne Forsythe, wrote the following for a 1993 Fortune Magazine article: "Adamson made what has been described as a thunderous entrance as CEO, telling employees at his first meeting that he was "going to do everything possible to provide better jobs for women and minorities. And I will fire you," he warned, "if you discriminate. Anyone who doesn't like the direction this train is moving had better jump off now." Within a few months of the change in management, all but four of the company's top twelve officers had left. Among those Adamson hired as replacements were a Hispanic man and an African American woman."

Evidence that systemic discrimination extends across the corporate landscape has come to light through history-making EEOC investigations, lawsuits, and settlements involving other corporate giants, as well, most notably Texaco and Coca-Cola. Record payouts reaching $170 million and far-reaching consent decrees mandating the monitoring and review of hiring by outside independent boards and regular reports to judges were hailed as a signal of the pending end to unfair and unequal treatment of protected-class individuals. Companies as much as cried uncle and began to implement far-reaching policies and initiatives to demonstrate they'd gotten the message loud and clear. As those historic cases and the companies involved faded from the spotlight, philosophers and pundits alike declared the war over.

However, in 2002, years after Denny's and others made history and before his Denny's book was published, Adamson made this observation to a reporter which was highlighted in an article for aboutdoubt.com related to race relations:

"I firmly believe that Denny's reflects most Fortune 500 companies. Diversity and inclusiveness is nothing more than a memo, as opposed to being part of the corporate culture." This came on the heels of new claims of discrimination years after he'd joined Flagstar and successfully instituted a broad cultural shift that eventually transformed Denny's into what it is today: a national leader in diversity.

Adamson's comment offered a view that the war was far from over; it had simply been reshaped and hidden behind public relations and marketing campaigns, complete with fancy brochures and policy manuals. Diversity training took center stage and companies established zero-tolerance policies under which anyone who discriminated was supposed to be subject to termination.

Years later, another CEO called out the systemic discrimination again. In 2005, Leonard Roberts, CEO of RadioShack, told a Fort Worth group of business leaders gathered to celebrate a diversity project, (an initiative set up by business leaders to develop programs to improve diversity in corporate America) that "the glass ceiling for people of diversity is still an unfortunate reality, including [at] our own company. Shame on every one of us who is or has been a CEO for allowing it to stand."

The story, which appeared in the *Dallas Morning News* on August 9, 2005, provided some background on Roberts's career-long struggle to eliminate discrimination in the workplace. Information included in the story detailed his short stint at Shoney's restaurants, where he promptly settled a discrimination suit after taking over as

CEO. According to various accounts, the Shoney's environment of discrimination had begun from the top with the founder. Not only wouldn't he hire African Americans, he fired any manager who did.

Unlike Adamson's situation, there was no publicity about Shoney's discriminatory culture, and Roberts wasn't told about the EEOC investigation of the company prior to taking over. When he found out and evaluated the depth of the problem, he made the move to settle the lawsuit. However, that action also resulted in his resignation.

The founder, who still owned a large chunk of the company's stock and was chairman of the board, insisted on Roberts's removal as a condition of settling the charges. His job was the price Roberts had to pay in order to see that the right thing was done. "You cannot fake it," Roberts has been quoted as saying. "You must stand up for what is right regardless. You cannot maintain your integrity 90 percent and be a leader. It's got to be 100 percent."

One of the companies participating in the gathering for the diversity project hosted by Roberts was my employer at the time, Kprints, Inc. Although his lead on diversity wouldn't filter down through the field ranks easily, it could be said that Jerry did it right personally and tried to get the company to do it right as well.

Within a year of taking over the reins as CEO in 2001, Jerry named a white female as executive vice president of operations. A minority female filled a regional vice president position, and an internal employee of Indian descent was promoted to the senior vice president and general manager of U.S. operations. Jerry transformed the executive suite from all-white males to a bastion of diversity.

Setting that example provided an opening and cover for others within the organization. One of the takers of Jerry's proposition, Sean, director of human resources, was able to get a little more aggressive when it came to enforcing and promoting the company's diversity and inclusion expectations. Another was Liz. For certain, such people were few, and Sean's overall forward-thinking ideals of how human resources should operate faced brick-wall resistance, despite Jerry's lead. For the most part, the culture of discrimination didn't come to an end.

As I look back at all the companies I have worked for, including those I have written about in detail in this book, with one exception the CEOs were like Jerry at Kprints: they preferred a culture of diversity and inclusion and sent that clear message to rank-and-file employees. However, none went as far as Jerry with action, and not even Jerry went as far as the decisive action demonstrated by Adamson. The one exception, Clint at Restaurant Group, fell into the Shoney's founder category.

Adamson not only focused on revenue and profits, as most new CEOs do, he also had a laser-focus on the culture. Maybe he would have been more conservative in his approach if he hadn't been backed up by the board of directors who, besieged by public outrage, gave him the mandate he needed. The fact is, he had that support and he acted decisively. Most CEOs don't, and as demonstrated by what happened to Roberts at Shoney's, it's a fair bet that most don't go as far as they would like out of fear of ending up the same way.

Leaders' lack of laser-focus often results in the continuation of the same culture that existed before they made their vision known. It's virtually guaranteed that there will be no recognition of the depth of the problem. It also guarantees that when an incident of discrimination or other unfair treatment arises, a less than aggressive policy will remain in place to deal with it. Therein is the reason that, despite how impressive Jerry's efforts were, they weren't enough to stem the tide of discrimination.

Jerry's management style, as he described years later in an article he wrote having to do with the subject of employee recognition, was " to hire the best people you can find and then get the hell out of their way." The problem with this philosophy, which we can assume is held by many in his position, is that some of those "best people" are either engaged in discriminatory hiring practices themselves or are hard-pressed to challenge anyone else who might discriminate, especially if it is common to the culture. They are affected by their own bias, peer pressure, association, and fear of not staying a member of the club of insiders.

Leaving the monitoring of the advancement of diversity and inclusion to those "best people" puts it in the hands of human resources. Historically, that department's overall and individual performance is evaluated with input from the sales and operations people they service.

Leaving investigation of discrimination complaints to those "best people" also means putting it in the hands of the legal department. That means one thing and one thing only: protecting the company from exposure. Part of the process of protecting the company is to ensure that any investigation is limited to that one incident. Equally, the system insures that remedies don't go beyond that one incident, thus maintaining the status quo by virtue of the fact that the broader implications to the culture are never considered.

CULTURE

This is one of the major reasons why systemic discrimination continues to exist. By the time a CEO or other top executive becomes aware of a particular incident that might cause them to take a closer look at the culture as a whole, it's too late. The spin has been filtered through the perpetrator, human resources, as well as legal. The CEO is inclined to trust those "best people."

Kelly Whitney, Managing Editor for diversity executive magazine wrote this in the July/August 2011 issue:

"attorney Patrick J. Boyd, partner at the Boyd Law Group PLLC, offered a candid assessment of the problems companies face establishing a culture of inclusion and diversity and making it stick. He stated he had observed passive-aggressive behavior in corporate America with regard to diversity, giving as an example the elaborate sixty- to seventy-page handbooks filled with policies and procedures companies come up with, designed to illustrate how they have embraced diversity and prohibit discrimination.

Boyd points out how these handbooks have little application, saying, "Employees likely won't read something that big, and therefore organizations tend to operate the same way they did before the policies were implemented."

Boyd also notes that the same has been proven true with mandatory diversity training to promote an inclusive workforce "if it's the only action taken." To illustrate this view, Boyd references a lawsuit he was working on against Hanes. His African American client Yunusa Kenchi was allegedly forwarded an e-mail written by a supervisor that read, "We should go forward with getting this nigger out of here." Kenchi was fired two days later. Within that two-day time frame, the person who sent the e-mail attended a diversity training session held by the company."

Whitney also quotes Boyd as saying "While I certainly don't think [discrimination is] something that any professional should be thinking about or worried about all the time, there's an equally great risk to presuming it's not there at all. The idea that now we have an African American president, this is a post-racial America, is naïve, and perhaps there are too many people who believe that is the case. I regret saying this, but, I think it must be said. Title 7, the Civil Rights Act of '64 passed more than forty-five years ago. Notwithstanding that, and the fact that we have an African American president, racism is alive, well, and existing in corporate America."

Individuals like the manager who sent the e-mail to Boyd's client permeate corporate America. Their victims aren't restricted to race. One could just as easily insert the words ageism and sexism. For that reason, I disagree with Boyd's statement that racism isn't something professionals should be thinking about all the time or worried about. All of us should be—especially those professionals within the corporate ranks responsible for running the business, like CEOs and other top executives. Even boards of directors who are responsible for selecting that next CEO should mandate that any new regime include as much focus on evaluation of the culture in this regard as it does productivity, revenue, and profits.

Without that focus, the old system is in play. When an incident of discrimination gets outside the company, either because of publicity, complaints to a government agency, or a lawsuit, the legal department goes into defense mode, as they apparently did with Boyd's client, despite even the most damning of evidence like the memo sent to Kenchi. That part of the system demands denial and litigation, as it did in the Texaco case, which was in full swing, and only came to an end after smoking-gun evidence became public. Until that point, even the CEO was powerless to do anything but go along with the legal battle.

The Kprints legal department's mandate was described during an HR training meeting in August of 2006. The corporate attorney said this: "It's our job to defend the company against claims of discrimination, whether we did it or not." All companies, including Denny's and RadioShack, have systems designed to defend the company against any manner of accusation, related investigations, and lawsuits.

OK, a corporation has a right to defend against allegations. Our legal system affords the same rights to corporations as individuals; you are innocent until proven guilty. But what if corporate staffers know the allegations are true? Is it really the right stance to defend the company regardless of how pervasive the situation, regardless of how devastating the acts? In defense of the company, is it reasonable to destroy evidence, silence witnesses, retaliate? Is it OK to cover up and otherwise manipulate the law and the process in order to defend what is morally indefensible?

What about dealing with employees who lie under oath or present such an outlandish explanation in their version of events that you know they are lying? What if the acts being defended involve sabotaging the brakes of a tractor-trailer operated by a female driver who complained about sexual harassment? What about manufacturing evidence or overlooking intimidation and threats of violence? What about murder? These are not fabricated or exaggerated possibilities. They actually happened.

What's maddening about this posture—fight tooth and nail, deny, and litigate—is that it doesn't have to be this way. The same laws companies spend so much time, effort, and money to protect against actually provide a path to doing the right thing.

The law recognizes and the courts have ruled that a company isn't liable if they take action to correct a problem once it becomes known. I contend that therein lies the reason for the shame Roberts put on CEOs. They don't take the action. The kind of zero-tolerance policies like the one Jameson initiated aren't enforced the way he enforced his. Lip-service is the rule of the day. As Jameson said, "Diversity and inclusion are nothing more than a memo."

I'll add "with a few exceptions," by virtue of the fact that Denny's, Coke, Texaco, and RadioShack voluntarily or by legal decree have shown the path to solving this problem forever.

The lack of diversity goes far beyond apathy or the lack of backbone of a CEO to stand up the way Roberts did. Because the law provides protection if a company takes action, yet they refuse to do so, I contend the lack of diversity is purposeful, it's growing, and it has the potential to affect everyone. As proof of this, I point again to the most recent job opening advertisements by employers which indicate that the unemployed are disqualified simply because they are unemployed. Companies are now asking for age and social security numbers during the application process, whereas prior to this recent economic and political climate the majority of companies only asked for these details after a job offer, and the disqualification of the unemployed was one of the secrets between hiring managers and recruiters.

More revealing is the resurgence of openness in regard to acts of discrimination as demonstrated by this recent article about Bass Pro Shops, which appeared in the *Huffington Post* on September 21, 2011:

The article informed us that Bass Pro Shops, one of the leading retailers of outdoor gear, is being sued by the U.S. Equal Employment Opportunity Commission for allegedly discriminating against African American and Hispanic applicants in several of its stores.

"Describing the lawsuit as both "major" and "nationwide," the EEOC alleges that the retailer discriminated against minority applicants, retaliated against employees who spoke out about what they considered unfair hiring practices, and destroyed internal records related to hiring. Certain non-white applicants, the agency claims, were not given jobs because they did not fit the Bass Pro brand.

Bass Pro has been discriminating in its hiring since at least November 2005," the EEOC said in a release. Minority job seekers, the agency said, were "routinely denied" positions as cashiers, sales associates, team leaders, supervisors and managers at Bass Pro stores. Managers at Bass Pro stores also made "overtly racially derogatory remarks" affirming the practices and noted that African American candidates "did not fit the corporate profile," the EEOC asserts. The alleged discrimination occurred at Bass Pro stores in Texas, Louisiana, and Indiana.

In a statement, the company said it was "extremely disappointed" in the agency's decision to file suit. The company said it fully cooperated with the investigation and denies the allegations. "This investigation and the EEOC's conduct demonstrate a troubling tendency by the EEOC to stereotype those who love outdoor sports and support conservation as people who unlawfully discriminate or oppose equal opportunity for all,"

Mike Rowland, vice president of human resources, said in a statement."

I was particularly intrigued by several specific revelations in this article: the fact that insiders blew the whistle, complained about discrimination, and were retaliated against; the statement that African American candidates "did not fit the corporate profile"; and the accusations of destroying documents. Did you catch that line where the Bass Pro representative attacked the EEOC, in broad strokes literally accusing them of stereotyping? It's the old accuse-the-accuser tactic, and even a federal government agency isn't immune.

Equally worth noting is the EEOC's claim that Bass Pro has been discriminating since 2005. It was November of 2004 when Abercrombie and Fitch settled a discrimination lawsuit, agreeing to pay over $40 million for similar violations of the law. They, too, were accused of profiling job applicants in line with what they believed their image was. Minorities were relegated to back rooms and shelf-stocking.

The main point here is that Bass Pro didn't get the message delivered through the outrage and public condemnation of the likes of Texaco, Coke, Denny's, or any of the other public cases that have found their way into the news. If anything, the allegations that specific instructions were openly given and strategy discussed tells us that employers have become more emboldened believing that, despite the history and lessons, there is a path to maintaining the white-male status quo.

Bass Pro isn't alone. The revelation of their situation, along with the companies I have worked for and the thousands of other cases that show up on websites seldom frequented by the general public, proves that what occurred before the civil rights movement of the sixties, what was the status quo in the seventies and eighties, what was said to be on its way out in the nineties, still flourishes and even right-minded, well-intentioned CEOs are the last to know.

There is hope in the fact that there were whistleblowers at Bass Pro, indicating that part of the paradigm seems to be shifting with new generations of employees who have a savvier understanding of rights and a tolerance of diversity and culture. However, the power of money, subterfuge, and retaliation continues to affect millions of job seekers and employees, thereby begging an answer to several observations and questions. This is what we face in the hunt for the job, the question I raise time and time again as a company goes to any length to defend the status quo and add new obstacles to keep qualified people out: how far do we go as job applicants? Do we, as job seekers, have an equal right to go to any length to get the minimum of a fair and equal opportunity for the job? Do I, as a corporate recruiter, have an equal right to work against my employer to ensure equal treatment of job applicants?

My answer is yes we do—but that's not all.

CHAPTER 18

Companies Lie

"*Every experience in life, everything with which we have come in contact in life, is a chisel which has been cutting away at our life statue, molding, modifying, shaping it. We are part of all we have met. Everything we have seen, heard, felt or thought has had its hand in molding us, shaping us.*" Orsen Swett Marden

As I write this, I am halfway through my fifty-fourth year. While I have hope that the future will bring me back to a more positive view, at this moment the chisel that has been cutting away at my life statue has brought me to this certainty: anyone who decides to pump up his or her resume, withhold information, or flat-out lie is justified. They are no worse or no better than the companies or employees they lie to. The managers—and, by extension, the companies—are, as Marden described so eloquently, "a part of all they have met, everything they have seen, heard, felt, or thought, [that] has had its hand in molding and shaping them."

By that reckoning, not only are hiring managers forged with their own bias, they have been modified, manipulated, and chiseled by others who have shown that the path to survival and prosperity requires them to lie, manipulate, and use the system as it is, thus perpetuating it.

The same experiences that forced me underground to avoid the wrath of retaliation force the hiring managers to assimilate into the system as it is. The corporate system demands it and all but promises to protect them if they go along with the status quo.

Whether the motivation is to maintain the status quo or cover up wrongdoing by a manager, hiring managers and companies lie. The lies and manipulation can be found in every aspect of the hiring and employment process. They can be found in corporate marketing and public relations designed to build a façade of diversity and inclusion that eventually adds to the company's defense should they be faced with the truth. It only gets worse as the stakes get higher, when companies have to respond to government agencies or investigators who seek to break the code and root out the truth.

Until the smoking gun—revelation of secret tape recordings in which executives discussed destroying evidence and making disparaging statements about African Americans and other minorities—Texaco denied the existence of systemic discrimination. Two of those executives eventually found themselves facing criminal charges for obstruction of justice.

At FSfoods in 1999, the smoking gun was a memorandum that read: "I can't believe we are paying this nigger more money than our white managers." Unfortunately, it didn't come to light until thirteen days after I agreed to a $240K settlement.

It's possible the reason they decided to settle was because someone knew the memo was out there and it could have blown my case wide open. I am more inclined to believe that cooler minds looked at the whole of the evidence gathered during the investigation and deposition process and realized that the longer the case went on revealing lies and cover-up, the worse it got for them.

Their case began to fall apart during the EEOC investigation process. The lie that termination of my employment was strictly a cost-saving measure didn't hold up against records obtained during the investigation. A few months prior to this decision, the company had spent thousands to outfit the Brookfield, Wisconsin, location with computers specifically for the recruiting department. The route service operations at the location were merged with another location on the other side of town, allowing my department to take over the entire building and thus save operations building expense that would fall on HR. The cost-savings analysis conducted by the company demonstrated the fiscal significance of maintaining and growing the department in Wisconsin.

When they announced my departure from the company, they named the new head of the department. Technically the title changed, but the job remained the same, proving it was a lie when they'd said my position was eliminated.

Company documents also dispelled claims of performance issues—their lie that I was never promoted to national recruiting manager, that I never complained about discrimination, and that discrimination didn't exist in the company. They couldn't explain their own documents, which showed a different picture.

The year I started with FSfoods, they reported the following numbers to the EEOC:

- The 830 sales managers included only two African Americans, two females, and six Hispanics.
- Of 56 key account managers, there was one African American, and five females
- Within the 6,059 route sales positions, which were the mandatory training positions for future advancement into operations and sales, African Americans held 29, and there were only 37 females.
- When it came to the 125 upper management positions, including division managers and regional managers, there were no minorities or females.

They overlooked the fact that my supervisor Todd had made a notation on a memo I faxed to him. They denied that anyone saw the itemized acts of discrimination. Yet, he'd faxed it back to me with the handwritten notation, "I'm passing it along."

A written agenda showing my presence proved they lied when they stated I never presented anything to the executive committee about the discrimination I witnessed. They lied when they claimed that I never reported discrimination and never had the conversation with Todd about the "lazy black people" comment. He swore under oath that I never threatened to go to the EEOC.

During his deposition, Todd eventually had to admit he'd lied under oath when he'd denied telling me about the route driver who'd sued because he'd been kept from getting a plum route. The driver's manager had explained, "I'm waiting for the right area to open up. I already know where it is. It's a salt and pepper area. You'll fit right in." That and another settlement, the result of a regional vice president refusing to consider an African American for promotion because he found out the driver was married to a white woman, were documented.

These and other discrepancies led the EEOC to determine that there was probable cause that I was retaliated against because I opposed discriminatory hiring practices. The lies made my case.

Although I was able to prove that I was retaliated against, the memo proved there was something much more sinister—beyond their fear that I was violating the code—already in the works.

Maybe my outburst did hasten their plan to move me out, but it became clear that my days were numbered as soon as the white powers that be found out I was making more money than they were. Not me in particular, but the black guy, the nigger. I was good, as long as I was in my place—below them.

The unleashing of the culture of discrimination to eliminate me began with one person. Todd. He engineered it. While I believe that, I don't think, for him, it was because I was black. He was one of the people who'd gone out on a limb to recommend they hire the black guy. He used the racist culture because he knew that it was the only way to get me out.

My performance was over the top. His words. Everyone saw that. His words. There was only one way to deal with the high-performance employee who made more money than him. He had to use the one thing that would override everything else. His weapon was the bigotry of those in power. He just had to get the ball rolling.

The Restaurant Group lied to the EEOC during its investigation, as well. They claimed the CEO didn't know I couldn't relocate and, therefore, my claim of retaliation was "totally without merit." A memorandum dated September 2007, highlighting his understanding that relocation was impossible forced him to backtrack. But he lied again, claiming he "forgot."

Twenty-four hours after receiving notice of the EEOC complaint they had changed their minds. I no longer had to move. "It was all a misunderstanding," they said. If I had made it clear that relocation was out of the question, they claimed, they would not have brought it up in the first place.

Pursuing a state or federal investigative process isn't necessary to gain the right to file a lawsuit. The value comes in hoping the evidence is compelling enough to warrant a wider investigation. Companies know this. It is the primary motivator for them to lie, manipulate the truth, falsify records, and generally cover up whatever is going on in the company. No matter what phase of the recruiting, hiring, or employment process, the culture of lies and deception is an intricate part of an overall strategy to protect the company from culpability and thus accountability.

In my early years of employment, before I became wise to the façade, I was an unwitting accomplice. I was relentless when it came to weeding out job applicants for the slightest infraction, based on whatever standard the company demanded. A lie had always been the worst infraction, allowing for no reprieve when the job applicant was found out. Equally, I had no reason to doubt the validity of the standards given for rejecting a job applicant. I operated with the belief that all job applicants were held to the same standard. Therefore, I upheld with unrelenting zeal even those standards that didn't make sense or defied reason and common sense—someone didn't dress right, they seemed to be a job-hopper, they made more money from their last job, or they lived on the wrong side of town.

Today, knowing the ugly truth, I can only advise job applicants to embark on the job-search process understanding, with a high degree of certainty, that managers and companies lie. The system is a lie, and the rules are a lie. Individuals who establish the rules, especially those which require applicants to tell the truth, and expect employees to conduct themselves with the highest level of integrity don't expect the same of themselves and haven't shown me that standard. They are not worthy of the respect of an individual's integrity. You are at a disadvantage if you don't understand that they lie.

What are they lying about?

- The most qualified person gets the job.
- You're overqualified. The truth is there is no such thing as being overqualified.
- None of your answers in the assessment will be used to determine your employability with the company.
- Your qualifications received fair consideration.
- We have decided to move forward with another candidate whose qualifications are a closer match to our needs.
- We don't discriminate.
- We are an equal opportunity employer.

- We thoroughly investigated the allegations in the complaint and found no evidence that discrimination occurred.
- There are no double standards when it comes to employment decisions.
- We didn't know, and it's certainly not company policy.

All of us would do well for ourselves by keeping this in mind and do whatever it takes to make it as hard as possible for them to add any one of us to their list of victims.

CHAPTER 19

HR Matters?

I confess that I have my own negative biases and prejudices, and there are times when I act on them. For instance, I believe that women are better people than men. They are smarter, more thoughtful, more shrewd, hold more conviction, and are more apt to do the right thing. Women work harder than men. Women are stronger and more reasonable. They are more trustworthy, loyal, and more willing and able to sacrifice for the good of others and right of cause. I cannot explain this bias any better than the person who has a negative opinion about minorities or holds an opposite view of women. Their excuse is my excuse—it has been my experience.

I also confess to a negative view of people who are in human resources. Similar to the way people stereotype all attorneys as nothing but bloodsuckers, I stereotype human resource people as nothing but inept drones. I use the same excuse—it has been my experience. Because of this bias, I am automatically suspicious of human resource people. Therefore, I am unrepentant when warning applicants that these are the last people they should trust at any phase of their hiring process or once they become an employee.

Generally, my experience has been that most HR people are, by their training or lack thereof, just as willing to go along with the status quo as they are, for their own benefit, to violate the rules, policies, and laws they are charged with upholding. They are more inclined to turn on the messenger to protect themselves and the company. They are apathetic. They cover up for those who discriminate, and they discriminate themselves.

I advise job applicants and employees alike to be extra-vigilant and hold HR personnel suspect at all times because, as a society, we have been programmed to believe that people who hold these positions are honest brokers when it comes to administration of policies and the law. We have been conditioned to believe that they will ensure that employees are treated fairly and that those in power will be held accountable when they abuse that power. With a few exceptions, my experience has been that the opposite is true.

I make these confessions as a means to excuse my failure to stick to my idea of taking people at face value.

In 1996, when it came to Todd, the lone human resource representative for a field organization of over nine thousand employees at FSfoods, the evidence of the cultural surroundings and his experience, training, and length of years with the company put me on guard.

Todd met me at the airport when I visited the corporate office for orientation on my first day. I didn't take at face value his proclamation that he was one of the good guys who wanted to see the company change from their history of discrimination to one of diversity and inclusion. I didn't take at face value his claim that he never understood the founder or the company's problem with African Americans. He bolstered his "color-blind" attitude by pointing out that his best friend, who'd worked alongside him when they were in field marketing, was African American. "We got along fine," he said.

Prior to getting the nod for the HR manager position the same week I was hired, he'd spent twenty-two years in marketing and sales. He'd started with the company like everyone did—he'd driven a delivery truck. He'd had no human resource experience when they'd tapped him for the job.

What he knew about hiring, employee relations, discrimination laws, or any other aspect of dealing with employees had come from his field experience as a member of the same group that, for the most part, had taken the founder's lead for more than fifty years.

During the ride from the airport, Todd provided a damning history of the company's discriminatory past, including condemnation of the company founder. According to him, if the founder of the company had still been alive, I wouldn't have stood a chance of getting the high-profile position of regional recruiter. There were few minorities and women in key roles. The rules were simple; with the exception of labor positions in the company's factories, an applicant had to be a white, Christian, Lutheran, conservative, Republican male. It was also preferred that the candidate was married with children.

Despite Todd's openness, I could not ignore the fact that he'd come from the ranks of those he was now charged with policing. As it turned out, as evidenced by his move to terminate my employment after my outburst about going to the EEOC, I was right about him.

While FSfoods' lack of HR scale necessary to meet the employee population left no question that HR didn't matter and that, if at all, change in the culture would be driven by the will and pleasure of operations management, the other companies I worked for went overboard in their attempts to create the exact opposite impression.

HR employees were prevalent at Kprints and Uniforms. But large numbers of HR people and policies on paper, including a policy of zero tolerance for discrimination, aren't any good if the corps of HR people are unable or refuse to uphold them. This was the case at these companies. If it were not for the blatant acts of discrimination perpetrated by some of them, they might have been successful with the façade.

One incident that is seared in my memory involved Paul, the executive vice president of human resources at Kprints. He approached me when I was standing in the main lobby of the corporate headquarters, looking at pictures of employees who had received recognition for their contributions to the company. It was called the Wall of Fame. I thought it should be called the Wall of Shame because some of the faces staring back at me belonged to managers who violated the CEO's directive of diversity and inclusion. One of them found a way to remove me from a recruiting assignment for his region when I questioned his refusal to consider a woman or a minority for a district manager position.

It had been one of those rare moments when I couldn't control my anger. By the VP's order, the HR director told me, after rejecting two females and a minority, that they no longer needed my help. His excuse was that they wanted to go with an outside recruiter who had local contacts. It was bullshit. The inference was that the candidates I'd sent weren't local, even though they were. The inference was that I had no local contacts, even though I did. That's the way recruiting works. Local candidates.

Paul asked, "So, are you trying to figure out how you're going to get on that wall?" It was as if I should admire those people and want to be one of them. Paul was fully aware of the problems with that particular manager.

I bring this up as a way of illustrating the concentration of superficial attributes and the lack of focus on serious issues that were prevalent in the environment. The execs operated in a bubble, unable or unwilling to see important problems. Paul didn't have a clue how bad some of those people were or how much they were hurting the company. What he did know didn't seem to matter. The company's attention to sales or profit numbers or an employee's participation in some community project that enhanced the company image overshadowed negative conduct, which, if exposed, would hurt the company.

The bubble skewed Paul's ability to see or understand what was going on right under his nose. He didn't see that one of his direct reports was part of the problem. I received an e-mail from Paul's direct-report Chris, a field HR VP. In the e-mail, he disqualified a district manager candidate in violation of laws barring discrimination based on marital status. The e-mail noted the candidate's recent divorce and his single-parent status. "I'm concerned he will have a conflict with time for work in view of the fact that he has small children to care for. Pass on him."

In California, the human resource director rejected an HR generalist candidate because the applicant was a single mother. The director explained her reason. "I know it's wrong, but I'm a single mother and I know how difficult it was for me to keep up with work and care for a small child—sick days and all that. I just can't afford to have someone with those kinds of needs." She also went along with her regional VP's decision to reject an African American candidate with more than ten years' experience as district manager because he "axed" a question instead of "asked." "That might be OK where he works at Best Buy in LA," she said, "but it will be a problem in northern California where we want to put him."

Nationwide, with the exception of Sean and Liz, HR staffers went along with whatever a hiring manager wanted to do. Any attempts I made to point out the lack of diversity or a pattern of unequal treatment of candidates depending on gender, age, or minority status was met with pro-corporate rebuttals. Some of them discriminated themselves and covered up despite the fact that the CEO had set a precedent through words and deeds that the rule of the day, any day, was inclusion and diversity based on the most qualified applicant for the job.

At Kprints, they undermined or simply ignored the CEO's directive. At Uniforms, human resources management took the CEO's directive of an open environment, defined by speaking up and challenging the status quo, to heart. Only they bastardized it, using it to identify dissenters and weed them out.

Despite my own warnings about HR people, I did selectively give them the benefit of the doubt although it was with apprehension. My decision to trust and confide in Terri, the other HR director who eventually jumped on the corporate bandwagon to help push me out of the company, was calculated. I viewed her with suspicion because of her HR management status—until she confided in me.

She volunteered a negative view of the company culture similar to mine. She predicted the final dismantling of what was left of the limited autonomy of human resources a year and a half before it occurred. It was right after Doug, the VP of field HR and the only person with the experience and fortitude to fight for HR equality in the power structure, was replaced by Liz. Terri began her job search shortly thereafter and sought my advice. She lamented the deterioration of structure as Liz and others in HR upper management fought and maneuvered to gain favor with operations and sales managers. Terri even voiced skepticism with the CEO's constant urging that employees at all levels speak up and challenge.

The only difference between gossipmongers and us was the fact that the information we shared wasn't gossip. As she shared her firsthand knowledge of who was up and who was down in the corporate structure, warned me about managers in her region who discriminated, and repeated comments of disdain toward Liz and Jennie, I shared confidential information provided to me by Liz.

Terri gave me advice on how to deal with the discrimination I witnessed, as well as the retaliation I experienced from Shitty and those who followed him. She applauded my decision to file an EEOC complaint. She agreed with my assessment of the discriminatory culture, especially as it related to the second-class status of women. When I told her about my shouting match with Liz, she related a similar situation she'd gone through with her and added, "I told you. Your friendship doesn't matter. Competence doesn't matter. She's power-hungry. She'll do whatever it takes to get ahead."

Given our like-minded opinions and equal desire to leave the company, I developed a false sense of security that she was the kind of ally I could count on. She turned on me when I complained to her and sought additional advice after I filed the EEOC complaint. I had proof that the number of people involved in retaliation had expanded from the North region management to Liz and everyone in the corporate structure, including the regional VP, Jim, whom she provided HR support to in the Midwest. As it turned out, Shitty and Jim were old military buddies. I proffered there was reason to believe that Shitty had shared my complaints against him with Jim.

My primary evidence was the fact that Liz reneged on a promise to provide additional support when she transferred me from the smaller North region to the Midwest. When it came to number of personnel, the Midwest was two and a half times the size of the North. At the time of the transfer, everyone agreed that one recruiter couldn't handle one hundred fifty-nine sales positions, let alone keep up with management openings. I agreed to give it a shot, with the understanding that the company would make adjustments if I got overwhelmed.

Terri was in on the conversation when Liz disavowed offering any such support. From my view, it was part of the overall strategy to create a situation where I wouldn't be able to meet performance measures and, thus, establish a reason for termination of my employment. I said as much to Terri, arguing that it was a stupid and totally transparent act of retaliation. "I wish they'd just fire me instead of all this underhanded bullshit," I said. That's when she turned on me. "Why don't you just quit?" she asked. The conversation went downhill from there. Expansion of my claims of retaliation put her in the middle of the controversy, and she went into defense mode.

Before the end of the day, she sent me this e-mail:

I also want to follow up on some comments you made in our conversation this morning. I know you were frustrated and I know you have said this before but I was surprised that you said you hope you get fired. I hope you were not serious when you said that as I value your help :-). You also made reference about wondering whether you are now having more positions to fill because of the charge against the company. This really concerns me and I don't know if you were joking here or not but that was a serious allegation. Brian, you need to tell Liz or Jennie or even George, the corporate attorney if you really believe that you have been retaliated against for filing the charge. I know I won't tolerate it and I am sure they would not either. I have not seen the charge, and I would certainly hope that no one has retaliated against you. Be that as it may, you have to take this to Liz, to Jennie or to George. If you don't, I will have to say something to them because I can't let that go. That comment really bothers me and I want to make sure that no one in my region would do such a thing.

So that I don't worry about this, please confirm that you will let them know if you feel you may have been retaliated against for filing a charge, ok, Brian?

Thanks.

Terri W, PHR
Regional Human Resources Director

From that day forward, Terri limited the content of her e-mails to corporate-friendly dialogue. Except for the phone conversation we had after I received that memo, she never spoke to me again without a witness present.

She also went along with demands by her VP to take me off plum recruiting assignments, limited my access to other hiring managers, and instructed HR representatives in her region to take over sales recruiting assignments without telling me.

By her memos and actions, no one would know that she voiced her frustrations with the company as a whole and individuals whom she'd described as deceitful, incompetent, and lacking basic common sense, if not for the phone conversations I recorded. The one most damning to her credibility came immediately after she sent me that e-mail. Shocked and disappointed by the memo, I called her to apologize and promised not to bring up my concerns again. She admitted sending the e-mail to cover her ass. We agreed that if it came up, we would both tell the same story—she didn't know about my EEOC complaint until that conversation.

The most interesting aspect of the situation with Terri is the fact that six months later she had a hand in writing my midyear performance review. The bulk of the manufactured performance issues and negative comments came from her. Two weeks prior to delivering the review with Kathy, she'd announced her resignation. Until that announcement, I'd actually sympathized with her change in posture toward me. She had to protect her job and future with the company. Why she still went along with falsifying my performance record goes back to my earlier comments of negative bias against HR people. Terri was willing to continue to go along with the status quo like one of those inept drones. The willingness was part of her training.

I maintain that same negative bias toward all HR people today. I understand that it is unfair, and I have to work on it because it is as ridiculous as the stereotype that all lawyers are bloodsuckers or that black people are lazy. There is also the fact that nine lower level HR representatives, some of whom I have mentioned previously in this book, fought the status quo. Despite their low-level status, allowing them the least amount of power to withstand any retaliation, they spoke up and challenged. However, considering the fact that the number is so small in relation to the number of those who did not speak out, eliminating my bias will continue to be, as it has been, a challenge.

For purposes of this writing and my ultimate goal to give job seekers as much information as I can to help them overcome unfair and discriminatory practices, I emphasize my warning, because it is better to be safe than sorry.

You will never know who the enemy is. What is known is that HR is designed to benefit the company. What is known is that it is more than likely that the HR people who are interested in making decisions based on fairness and honesty and consistent application of laws and policy are under constant duress in a corrupt environment, if they have been allowed to keep their jobs at all.

JOB WARS

Job applicants are warned to be careful about what they divulge during the application and interview process. HR people are programmed to protect the company, including weeding out people who aren't a fit for the environment or who may cost the company money because of a disability or past medical problems. HR people are not on your side. They are not fair arbitrators of policy or the law.

CHAPTER 20

Kathy Milton

The story told us, "In October of 2010, a black television news technician filed a lawsuit against Fox News. Harmeen Jones charged that he was fired for complaining about racism. According to a *Huffington Post* article of October 20, 2010, the complaint alleged that several of the defendants "continually made racist, sexist, and extremely offensive comments throughout the course of every working day. These comments concerned African Americans, Arabs, Muslims, Hispanics, women, and Jews."

The *New York Daily News* reported on October 20, 2010, that Jones said he complained to the human resources department at News Corporation, which owns Fox News, in 2009. His colleagues responded by calling him a "snitch." After his complaints got back to his immediate managers, he was called in by his boss, who allegedly said, "We gave you a chance and you repay us by making complaints to HR? You're terminated." Jones also stated that he approached fellow African American employees to discuss what was happening. They told him he needed to keep his head down and not say anything.

I can more than just imagine how Jones must have felt when those fellow African American employees essentially told him to shut up. Bewilderment, rage, disappointment, fear, hopelessness, and despair all come to mind.

Equally, I am bewildered by my contradictory feeling of envy versus contempt and loathing for anyone who has the capacity to keep his head down and not say anything the way those African Americans advised Harmeen to do.

I wonder how different my life would be if I had the capacity to look the other way. Since I haven't, not for lack of trying, the exception I take to those individuals who have taken that route as members of a protected class is biased.

I believe members of a protected class have a special obligation to stand up and be counted. There is no limit to the number of times I ask, "Don't they understand that if it affects one, it affects all? How does anything change if we don't speak up and challenge?" Still, their reluctance to end up like Jones is understandable. Better to keep your mouth shut and get a paycheck so you can feed your family. However, what isn't understandable are those from a protected class, like Kathy Milton, who join in and help to either cover up what happens to people like Jones or who actually participate.

Kathy Milton is a pseudonym for two people from two different companies. They are both African Americans.

One is a female, the other is male. One is a recruiter, the other is a human resource manager. They have another trait in common. They both conducted themselves in a way that would easily earn them the label of "Uncle Tom" or "Oreo." Besides helping perpetrate discrimination against people of her race, Kathy has the additional distinction of supporting discrimination, intimidation, and harassment of women.

I know the Oreo label is harsh. And believe me when I say I am reluctant to describe anyone that way. From UrbanDictionary.com: "To much of the public, an Oreo is simply a black cookie sandwich with white cream filling. In the African American community, however, an Oreo is used as a racial slur to insult blacks that 'act white' or identify as such. The racial name Oreo is controversial because many blacks recount being called the racial term for doing well in school or speaking proper English, not because they didn't identify as black. In short, these African Americans were singled out as sellouts simply for excelling academically and in other areas. Many blacks find this term hurtful, for they are proud of their African American heritage."

The misuse of this term has expanded over the years. People like Secretaries of State Condoleezza Rice and Colin Powell have, unfairly, been described that way simply because they are Republicans. They became more suspect when they decided to serve in the Bush administration. The apprehension and mistrust of Bush by African Americans is evidenced by the less than 6 percent vote he received during the 2000 and 2004 elections.

There have been times when I've been described as an Oreo myself. The last time, I was in junior high school. There were maybe thirty blacks who attended besides my brothers and me. They stuck together like glue, refusing to associate with anyone of a different race. The people I hung with included A. Puente and my best friend N. Yashiro. Then there was my white girlfriend, Sue. It was my refusal to disassociate myself with those who didn't look like me that brought out the "Oreo!" cracks if I so much as nodded at another black. The ringleader of the taunting was a kid by the name of Pat—until a basketball game during gym class when we were paired together as guards on the same team.

Pat had an unbelievable jump shot that seldom missed the net from mid-court. So during that game, whenever I drove inside, instead of trying for the layup I'd catch him with a pass after he'd crossed the mid-court line. He would pivot and then let it fly. There was nothing but net every time.

We beat the pants off the other side, and from that day on, I was as black as he was. Never mind the fact that I had already demonstrated my "blackness" as student council vice president. I was the lone voice advocating for student activities that included African American history and culture. In the end, it came down to something as insignificant as playing basketball and passing off to the fellow black kid.

The Oreo and Uncle Tom labels only lasted for a short while, however, those three or four weeks I was labeled as someone who was black on the outside but white on the inside simply because I mixed with others besides blacks, cut deep. And so, I have been cautious not to label anyone else that way. Even when their actions might warrant it.

However, actions I have observed over the years have rekindled a newfound appreciation for the term. I have, for that purpose, come up with my own definition to justify its use. It's reserved for African Americans who, by their actions, harm other African Americans. In corporate America, it's reserved for those who discriminate against other African Americans or who are otherwise willing participants in cover-up or provide comfort to individuals who or a culture that discriminates.

Milton labeled himself as pro-black. He brought it up several times during the six months we worked together at FSfoods. It was a peculiar proclamation for someone who was visibly African American. The first time was during the interview process for the job in which, if hired, he would become my counterpart for the wholesale business unit of the company. I had my hands full as national recruiting manager with the thirteen thousand route sales reps in constant flux. I warned him about the culture where blacks had a hard time gaining entry and that he would hear things that might be upsetting.

It wasn't long before Milton found himself confronted with the same negative comments about African Americans that I did. During a regional meeting in Ohio that included managers from southern Indiana, West Virginia, and parts of Kentucky, one of the managers openly discussed the familiar inability to hire blacks for routes because white customers wouldn't accept a black person coming to their door. At one point, he defended his thinking, saying, "I'm actually doing you people a favor, because if I did hire you, there's a good chance you'd get shot the minute you stepped out of your truck." Beyond explaining the illegalities of making a hiring decision on those terms, I spent months pushing the idea that it was up to the individual to decide whether he wanted to put himself in a situation where he might get shot.

At that meeting and throughout the time we worked together, Milton took the side of managers like that, undermining the equal employment opportunity I advocated for blacks and others. He applauded a manager in Illinois who bragged about the way he showed women the job would be too difficult for them by creating a physical test that didn't apply to male applicants.

The delivery trucks were equal in size and shape to a midsize U-Haul moving vehicle. They had frozen-food cubicle doors on the side near the very top. A running board allowed the route person to step up and reach in to select items. There were also handles along the side and top. The manager would take the female applicant out to the truck and tell her she had to reach in with one hand and select six items from two separate compartments while holding onto one of those handles with one foot extended away from the running board. According to him, not one woman had the body strength to hold herself up long enough to gather all six items. Then, for good measure, after the applicant came down exhausted and unsuccessful, he'd tell her to imagine herself out on a rural road in the dead of winter with wind and arctic air whipping at her face.

As far as Milton was concerned, the manager was right to put women through that test. He agreed the job wasn't right for women, whether they wanted it or not. He believed those managers were right deciding to hire based on race in relation to the racial makeup of the customer base they served.

Instead of acknowledging that the lack of diversity in the company was based on discriminatory acts, Milton offered an opinion that fed into the stereotype that black people were lazy. He offered the opinion that the lack of employee hires was due to a lack of minority applicants. It was the same argument that managers made, including those who were caught throwing away applications from all the minority job applicants they'd claimed hadn't applied.

Milton claimed the lack of minorities at FSfoods was because of the lack of interest in the job itself. It was one of those jobs that was beyond the reach or expectations of most black people. He cited high income and the difficulties of commission sales as conditions blacks didn't generally aspire to. This was an amazing statement considering the fact that the average pay was in the mid-forty thousands. The comment went toward understanding how far he was willing to go to build his rapport within the company and destroy mine.

His negative take on the drive and ambition of black people gave comfort to the enemy. It reestablished doubt as to whether management was being discriminatory at all and generally gave the company reason to take no real action to end the practice. Beyond providing that comfort, a regional vice president who initially opposed the idea of hiring minorities but eventually became a fan alerted me to conversations Milton engaged in behind my back. Milton trashed me at every turn while providing anyone who would listen the kind of advice that would help them protect themselves from discrimination and labor laws. He even went as far as to play on their prejudice. He made the observation that he thought it was strange that a black man supervised an all-white staff, referring to me and my recruiting team.

A black going against the interest of other blacks is nothing new. The history books are filled with stories of slaves turning in other slaves who talked of escape. There were the house niggers who considered themselves better than field hands because they literally worked or lived in the house alongside the master and cared for his children. Their loyalty was to the white master.

Modern society has brought us a long way, but there is no shortage of African Americans who have earned their seat at the table by denying the existence of racism. I have come across very few who were as deep into it as Milton. In the course of my legal battle with the company, Milton went as far as providing an affidavit contradicting my version of the culture we worked in.

I was certain I would never come across the likes of someone like him again—until I met Kathy twelve years later at Uniforms.

Milton was motivated by a desire to get a seat at the table—my seat. Kathy's motivation was to keep hers. She advanced in level of authority for no other reason than by default. As Liz moved up, those who reported to her moved up, as well, regardless of whether they were qualified.

In the beginning, I felt sorry for Kathy. If it wasn't something as ridiculous as how she sat, Liz pointed out real deficiencies on a regular basis. It wasn't fair because Liz was the one who continued to promote her and thus put her in positions where she didn't have the ability to do the job.

When I first saw Kathy in action, I thought it was just incompetence. I gave her the benefit of the doubt because of a conversation we had a little over six months into my employment at Uniforms. According to her, the senior vice president had impressed upon a group of managers that they needed to get some diversity in their business units, which was a first. We had heard such statements before as standard fare during human resource meetings, but never directly from operations. Kathy said, "Maybe things will start to change around here!"

However, it wasn't long after when she did the number on Melissa mentioned in an earlier chapter. Other minorities and women fell victim to her willingness to manipulate the truth in order to either cover up or justify discrimination. There were just as many instances of sexual harassment and hostile work environment. That's what earned her the labels of Oreo and Mrs. Uncle Tom by others. For me, it became personal. Kathy was one of the HR directors who harassed me during the months leading up to my mid-year performance review. She was one of the HR directors who manufactured information about my performance. She spearheaded the strategy of retaliation during those months leading up to my forced resignation.

To be fair, I'll point out that Kathy's manipulation of the criteria for evaluating my performance may have also been motivated by revenge. After all, I threw the first blow when I discussed her lack of competence with Jennie during that meeting in August. For all I know, Jennie, despite assuring confidentiality, shared the details of that meeting with her.

Even if Kathy wasn't brought into the loop, I made the mistake of mentioning I'd spoken of her a few days after Liz left the company. Her reaction was unforgettable. The only thing I related to her was the fact that she was one of the people I talked to about my problems with Shitty. She responded by saying, "Sometimes I don't get you. Here I am keeping my head down, trying to keep a job and take care of my family, and you are out there mentioning my name."

If only that was all Kathy was doing, following the advice offered by those African Americans to Harmeen Jones, I might have felt guilty about mentioning her name. However, the lost jobs in the wake of her cooperation with managers who harassed women employees and discriminated against race, age, and gender demonstrated she was doing much more than that.

On the last day of my employment, I had to conference with her a last time. At the end of the call, she wished me luck, to which I replied, "Go to hell!"

CHAPTER 21

Fight Tooth and Nail

One of the best illustrations of how far companies will go to deny, litigate, and essentially fight tooth and nail rather than own up to any level of accountability came from a series of news stories that appeared in 2003 regarding the murders at defense contractor Lockheed Martin. The following information was taken from in depth coverage and follow up provided by ABC news Primetime reporter, Brian Ross, in 2005.

"Two black workers, Thomas Willis and Lynette McCall, had complained to management about fellow employee Doug Williams's racist remarks. "He said he was going to come in one day and kill a bunch of niggers and then kill himself." In one incident, Williams, a known racist at the plant, chose to leave work rather than remove a head-covering resembling a Ku Klux Klan hood. Booker Stevenson told a reporter from the *Clarion Ledger* of Jackson, Mississippi, that five years earlier, Williams had threatened to kill a half-dozen black employees after an argument over interracial dating.

After years of these and other threats and slurs against blacks at the plant, on July 8, 2003, Williams followed through by shooting and killing six coworkers—five of them black, including Willis and McCall—and wounding eight others before turning the gun on himself.

According to documents obtained by ABC News, Lockheed Martin knew about Williams but took very little action to deal with him. Yet, Lockheed management vehemently denied discrimination was any part of their culture and denied that the killings were even race-related. Lockheed's solution was to force Williams to take a diversity and anger management course. Those very courses, some would say, pushed him over the edge to make good on his threats."

As details of the incident raged in the press, the ABC reporter who investigated the story confronted Lockheed's CEO. The journalist was able to catch up to the CEO as he walked into a shareholders meeting. The CEO stuck to the company line—he said there was zero tolerance for discrimination at Lockheed Martin and the killings were not race-related.

According to recent updates in the news, Lockheed has been successful in limiting its exposure. The shooting victims and their families earlier sued the company, claiming Lockheed's management knew employee Doug Williams's racist views had created a volatile work environment but did too little to defuse the situation. The lawsuit sought unspecified damages.

The U.S. Equal Employment Opportunity Commission investigated the shooting and said Williams created a "racially charged atmosphere" at the plant. Lockheed Martin said its management had no way of knowing that Williams would go on a shooting spree and asked the court to consider the case under workers' compensation guidelines.

A federal appeals court ruled that the lawsuit against Lockheed Martin was a workers' compensation case. The designation, which Lockheed fought for, under Mississippi law limits damage awards to about $150,000 for each victim.

Some argued Lockheed's motivation was money. The defense contractor risked losing government contracts if it was found the company didn't meet equal employment standards. Potentially, billions of dollars were at stake. It's worth noting that while the company continues to deny discrimination is a part of their workplace, since that incident and the related litigation accusations, lawsuits, and settlements due to alleged mistreatment of employees at Lockheed have continued. Here's a sampling from EEOC government website:

Jan 14, 2009 Class action lawsuit alleges sex discrimination against female employees.

Jan 2, 2008 Lockheed Martin agrees to pay $2.5 million to settle a race discrimination and retaliation suit.

Apr 8, 2008 Lockheed Martin to pay $773,000 in age discrimination suit.

Lockheed isn't alone. A list of companies embroiled in cases of discrimination of one kind or another can be found on the EEOC government website and could be classified as the who's who of corporate America from just about every industry, including Federal Express, Walgreen's, Boeing, Walmart, McDonald's, and AutoZone. The list is endless, and while it continues to grow, many of the same companies appear on it again and again. And these are just the ones that are reported, usually for issues related to employees after hire.

That the Lockheed murders and the company's subsequent denial that the incident had anything to do with a discriminatory work environment, as described by the EEOC, came years after the discrimination lawsuits against Texaco, Coke, and Denny's makes them all the more tragic. Yet, opinions that the company failed to learn from the lessons of those other companies isn't exactly true, and I question whether Lockheed and others aren't simply motivated by money or loss thereof. There were really two lessons to learn from Texaco. The lesson companies may have taken more stock in is the one that showed them they could, depending on the circumstances, fight tooth and nail and fend off any level of liability or scrutiny.

At the very least, deny and litigate was the strategy Texaco followed amidst one the worst publicly scrutinized race discrimination cases in U.S. history. And apparently, destruction of evidence was part of the game plan by some in the organization.

According to some observers who followed the story, it was only after Texaco executives were caught red-handed using racially insulting language as they discussed the destruction of evidence that Texaco Chairman Peter I. Bijur did a flip-flop from his stance that systematic discrimination didn't exist at Texaco.

In what some called a textbook feat of corporate damage control, he agreed to spend $176 million to end the lawsuit filed by black employees whom Texaco had been stonewalling for years. The deal included an independent equality and tolerance task force to oversee changes in Texaco's employment policies. The task force would, in effect, be Texaco's in-house anti-bias agency, with access to all corporate records, and report to the board of directors. Max Berger, one of the plaintiffs' lawyers, said at the time, "The independent task force we have created will not only have the power to eradicate institutional discrimination at Texaco but also provide a model for corporate America to follow."

Three years later in 2000, although Coca-Cola initially denied allegations in a class-action lawsuit filed against them by four current and former African American employees for racial discrimination, Coke eventually agreed to a $192 million settlement, the largest ever in a corporate racial discrimination case. With that, they agreed to monitoring by an independent panel similar to what was instituted at Texaco.

These and other high-profile cases— and the resulting money paid out—provides some evidence that companies are better off admitting the wrongdoing quickly, and, thus, it is questionable whether defense and litigation is motivated by money alone. There is one common denominator when you look at these cases, as well as the situations I have found myself in over the years: all these companies hired minorities and women, to some degree. In every case, it was either limited to a few tokens like me, or, in cases where there were a number of minorities and women, there were limitations as to where they could work, what jobs they were able to hold, and how many were allowed to advance.

In 1948, singer and actor Nat King Cole, when describing the refusal of national corporations to sponsor his color-line-breaking variety show, said, "Madison Avenue is afraid of the dark." It was a clever metaphor describing white society's fear of African Americans and how major consumer brand corporations catered to that fear, believing that sponsoring the first show hosted by an African American might alienate or offend white customers in the Southern states.

By the 1990s, signs were everywhere that corporate America was still operating with a similar mentality. Although companies found a path to hiring minorities and women, the limitations that some called "window dressing" has been described by others as a Jim Crow mentality.

There were the smaller regional or statewide companies, like the real estate development firm in Florida that came under scrutiny when one of their recruiters made public the discriminatory statement by one of their sales managers. It was another one of those situations where the sales manager for the real estate company decided that the recruiter working for them, although an African American, would go along with the discrimination simply because she was an employee and therefore one of them.

The incident surrounded an applicant for a sales job who happened to be female and African American. The recruiter recorded conversations with the sales manager as they discussed the minority candidate. According to the recruiter, the sales manager was willing to hire the candidate but not for sales in the area where the company had what was considered prestigious, upscale property. "We can't have a black person in that area," he told her. "Let's hire her for our other property." The development property he had in mind was less upscale and considered more diverse in relation to the homebuyers it would attract.

That story made the national news as if it were something unusual. But the story regarding Friedman's Jewelers, with over six hundred fifty stores across the United States, never gained that spotlight. The information below was taken from www.gdblegal.com, the website for California law firm Goldstein Demchak Balle, Borgen & Dardarian.

"Friedman's is operating in a Jim Crow world," said Thomas A. Warren, counsel for the plaintiffs. "The corporate office forces managers to base their hiring, firing, and promotion decisions on the most appalling racial stereotypes. This kind of blatant discrimination cannot stand. It's wrong and it's illegal."

"Limiting the number and authority of African Americans and other minorities, "Friedman's has systematically discouraged African Americans from seeking promotions and from becoming too large a part of its workforce," said Morris J. Baller, lead attorney and partner at Goldstein, Demchak, Baller, Borgen & Dardarian, one of the law firms representing the plaintiffs. "This company has a corporate policy to impose a quota limiting the number of African American employees in any given store and has retaliated against managers who have attempted to hire and promote qualified African Americans."

"An audiotape of a conversation between division vice president Jack Steele and plaintiff Rondall Mitchell, a white man, who was in charge of twelve Friedman's stores, underscores the allegations in the complaint. Steele says: "Largo [Maryland store] is a piece of s----. On the tape, which was made with Steele's knowledge, Steele uses racial epithets, makes disparaging remarks about African Americans' appearance and ability, and demands that Mitchell hire fewer African Americans and fire existing black employees. Mitchell refused to comply with Steele's demands and was demoted and eventually left the company after being subject to retaliatory harassment.

The lawsuit alleged Friedman's discriminates against African American employees by:

- Explicitly limiting the number of African Americans hired and rejecting qualified African American applicants for store associate and store manager jobs.
- Denying qualified African Americans promotions to management positions above store manager.
- Using discriminatory criteria to make compensation, hiring, and promotional decisions.
- Maintaining an all-white higher level management despite having African American employees qualified for and interested in such jobs."

The Friedman's case underscores the fact that other companies that have made the headlines because of discrimination complaints are only a small part of the overall picture. The facts are as clear as day. The corporate landscape is filled with companies with diversity issues. The facts are in the number of women who are paid less than men for doing the same job, a totally outrageous disparity considering, again, the times we live in. The number of unemployed blacks and Hispanics is as high as ever.

Yet, all these companies are more apt to fight tooth and nail against these allegations, and it's my belief that it is more about protecting the Jim Crow culture. This is applicable to corporate America in general, and it can be argued that companies fight tooth and nail, deny and litigate, in order to protect this paradigm that has expanded beyond discrimination based on race and gender, but also age, disability, sexual orientation, religion, and medical status.

I contend that it was a Jim Crow mentality that kept minorities and women at a minimum at FSfoods, Kprints, the Restaurant Group, and Uniforms.

The answer to the other question—how companies get away with it for so long—is more complicated in that there is no single answer. If we look at the details of the Lockheed case, where they were able to convince a judge that the murders there fell into the workers' compensation category, the law played a role. When we look at other cases, like Texaco, Coke, and Denny's, we have to wonder how far any of those companies would have gone in the litigation process if not for the public scrutiny or smoking guns that came to light.

Part of the answer is in the way companies limit public and internal exposure. The less people involved in a case, the less likely other employees will come forward with damning information. Companies get away with protecting the Jim Crow world because of people like me who are compelled by duty or loyalty or fear of retaliation to work within the system in their attempt to change it. Companies get away with it because there are too few people like Mitchell from Friedman's who are willing to come forward. Even Mitchell, by all accounts, came forward – filing a complaint with the EEOC - only after he was directly affected.

Concluding that corporate America, by choice, prefers to fight tooth and nail isn't difficult when we look at all the advice and information available that offer an alternative. Here's some advice I found for employers on the Internet:

"Beware expanding EEOC investigation after employee complains about discrimination. Take every internal discrimination complaint seriously—and take quick action, too. Why? If the employee doesn't think your response was adequate, an EEOC complaint will probably follow. And that can spell big trouble if the EEOC decides to expand its investigation beyond the specifics of the original complaint. Then, instead of dealing with a single employee, you may find yourself looking at a class action.

"Case in point: Shelly M. was accepted into a management training program with a food purveyor. Soon, Shelly M. complained that a male manager insisted on referring to her as 'woman' and that other managers were e-mailing offensive material back and forth. After Shelly complained, the training director told her she was not 'demonstrating leadership skills' and that she wouldn't graduate from the program. No one with the company treated her complaints seriously, so she quit and then went to the EEOC.

"The EEOC expanded its investigation to cover sex discrimination throughout the company's training program. Then it issued subpoenas for detailed information on several employees."

FSfoods went to court asking to have the investigation scaled back to Shelly's original sexual harassment complaint, but the court refused. As of July 2011 the company faces allegations it engaged in systemic sex discrimination.

Final note: FSfoods could have short-circuited this lawsuit by taking Shelly's complaints seriously and banning offensive communication. All companies have the same option.

CHAPTER 22

Ambiguous Shades of Gray

It's a simple proposition, one we all come to understand early regardless of our lot in life: go along to get along. Keep your mouth shut and your head down. The rules apply differently and for different reasons depending on who you are and what you look like.

If you are a woman or minority, you are expected to follow that code while also accepting whatever abuse might come your way. It's the price you pay for the privilege of being allowed in at all.

The promise is that you will be allowed to exist, maybe advance, but just don't expect to rise above your station, and, in fact, be grateful for whatever you do get. You are even expected to be grateful despite the fact that only a token few advance within the company and you are not one of them, in spite of your skills and ability. Regardless of what you look like, if you violate the code, dare be the orphan boy Oliver and ask for more, you had better be ready to suffer the consequences.

Not only did Federal Express truck driver Marion Shaub dare to ask for more by expecting that she would be able to do a job historically held by men, she violated the code when she complained about the abuse she suffered simply because she was a woman. The consequences? On several occasions the brake lines to her tractor-trailer rig were loosened, cut, or filled with dirt. In each instance, it was only Shaub's extraordinary truck-driving skills that allowed her to retain control of her vehicle and avoid serious injury or property damage.

Other acts of retaliation from fellow employees and supervisors were designed to make her time at work as difficult as possible and affect her job performance so she would either quit or could be terminated. Her route assignments were changed, and the standard assistance of loading trucks provided to all tractor-trailer drivers was taken away from her.

This all happened after she made numerous complaints about gender-based hostility in her work environment. In the EEOC complaint, there were allegations that she was subjected to "anti-female remarks" from her male coworkers, including a comment that women should be "barefoot and pregnant" and that she "looked like a porn star." One male colleague allegedly told Shaub that if she were his daughter, he would "abort her."

A jury awarded Shaub $3.2 million, including $2.5 million in punitive damages. A little over a year earlier, Kathleen Talbot-Lima had been awarded $2.3 million after she was retaliated against for making a similar sexual-discrimination complaint against the company.

Ted Maines wasn't asking for more for himself. His violation of the code came in the form of protesting the actions of one of his brethren. The following account of his ordeal was provided in an EEOC press release on December twelfth 2004.

"When he saw that FedEx management was engaging in what he believed was discrimination, he thought calling the legal department was the right thing to do. For that, Maines said, "I was met with harsh retaliation by corporate management which nearly ruined my life and career."

A week after Maines complained, he was given an ultimatum: either accept a demotion of five pay grades and report to his subordinate or be issued a warning letter and face immediate termination for any subsequent "mistake." When Maines advised the company that he could not accept either option, Federal Express immediately issued a disciplinary warning letter containing a threat of termination. Thereafter, Maines was subjected to intense scrutiny, including electronic monitoring. He believed that his phones were monitored and his work subjected to a heightened level of review."

Maines ended up resigning from his position.

The "mistake" Maines made that led to what a federal jury would determine was retaliation and for which it awarded him $1.5 million in damages wasn't that he reported discrimination that he'd experienced personally. Maines, a white male, enjoyed the upward mobility of hard work and playing by the rules. He'd advanced from phone operator into management over his career with FedEx. He had no axes to grind, and it was also clear that if he would have just kept his head down and mouth shut he would have remained on the same track. He didn't have to stand up for the victims, two minority employees—one African American and one Hispanic—whom he'd promoted to supervisory roles. He didn't have to challenge the regional vice president who rescinded the promotions and gave the job to a recently hired white female.

Few cases of discrimination and related retaliation are as clear-cut as these examples. As Paul M. Barrett wrote in his book *The Good Black*, most discrimination cases are tinged in ambiguous shades of gray.

At Uniforms, there were no threats of termination. No performance write-ups. There were no outward signs of sabotage of my work equipment and no monitoring of my duties, at least not in the beginning. The changes in how I was treated were subtle enough to create that ambiguous shade of gray. To evaluate the situation from the outside, one would have to understand the significance of communication between hiring managers and the person charged with conducting their recruiting to understand the significance of the excommunication. One would have to know the significance of an outside contract recruiter getting direct access to hiring managers, as well as the importance of that recruiter knowing more than the company's internal recruiter.

Much of the retaliation I experienced was ambiguous enough to be explained away. Indeed, the company would attempt to do just that when they had to respond to the EEOC.

But I had a witness to the cultural environment who I believed would help prove my case.

The service manager at the New Jersey location complained to Karen, the HR representative, about the presentation I'd given five months earlier. As Karen put it, he went on and on about how it was terrible that I would talk about the lack of diversity to "a room full of white guys." His attitude, she said, was that of contempt. There was no question in her mind it was because I was black and "how dare you?" Providing me with this information and backing it up in writing was the catalyst for my move to file an EEOC complaint of discrimination and retaliation for opposing discriminatory hiring practices.

At Uniforms, those shades of gray were shrouded in a fog that included a narrative from the company, in response to the EEOC inquiry, in which they praised my performance and claimed to look forward to my continued success with the company.

My attorney pointed out that their explanation of the sequence of events was manufactured and he provided documents and access to witnesses that will eventually result in a successful prosecution of the case. As of this writing, those shades of gray have brightened a bit as the company, in their zeal to successfully force me out, have provided additional evidence that will go a long way in obtaining a ruling of probable cause when the case is finally heard.

At Uniforms, an HR representative provided a smoking gun of sorts. However, it will take getting people under oath in depositions and a subpoena of records to find out who knew what when. In stark contrast to the way FSfoods expanded their reasons for terminating my employment,

Uniforms stuck to one argument in their denial that discrimination existed and that I was retaliated against. We provided documentation that they manufactured information in order to make their case; the initial determination by the Wisconsin Equal Rights Division was no probable cause. Although as of this writing an appeal hearing is pending before a judge, Uniforms won the first round.

CHAPTER 23

White Guys Too

At Nonprofit Inc. the assistant store manager job we were interviewing for was twelve job levels below the director of operations position held by my boss, Scott. His area of responsibility encompassed retail operations, production, transportation, and several other departments, all with managers who reported to him and were certainly part of a long line of qualified successors that trumped the advancement of a lowly assistant store manager. As a participant in the management development program, Scott was on track for a position as president of a Nonprofit unit somewhere in the world. His rise to director of operations came as a consequence of the promotion of the person who hired and promoted me to sales manager, Gary.

Scott and I assumed our new roles at the same time. With only two stores and a third on the way, my role as sales manager wasn't a huge job. However, it was the type of position I'd dreamed of, using my retail business experience in an environment where it was about helping people instead of profits.

I'd come into the organization a little over a year earlier, taking over the smaller of those two stores. It had been failing to the point where there was talk of moving it from the current location. I was given credit for doubling sales in that first year. Because of the dire outlook, the increase was considered nothing more than miraculous and resulted in the promotion to manage both locations.

Although some of the growth can be attributed to cleaning up the store, reorganizing it to look like a regular retail outlet, and enhancing marketing to broaden the customer base, those changes didn't account for all of the "miraculous" recovery. I would argue the bulk of it occurred by accident.

A few days after taking over, I was introduced to two police officers. One of them came into my office with my assistant manager, Bob, and plopped some money down on the desk. Bob pointed to a cart of portable televisions that were headed to the trunk of the officer's patrol car. The officer owned an electronic resale store on the side. Nonprofit was one of his suppliers. Under an agreement with the last store manager, he was allowed to pay five cents on the dollar for merchandise, compared to what we would price the goods on the retail floor for the general public. On top of that, he was able to go through all the products as they were unloaded from the truck—in short, able to take anything that was salable (which meant it worked).

That was the day I established new rules that would apply to all merchandise and all customers: nothing is sold out of the backroom, nothing is sold out of stock carts, and nothing is sold without a price tag. It had to be on the shelf before it could be purchased.

I remember the discussion with the police officer when I told him I couldn't accept his money. It included some reference to how he provided special protection to the store, which amounted to him driving by several times a day. Occasionally, he would walk through the store on his way to the back room. That so-called protection, he warned, could come to an end. I remember Bob pulling me to the side and also warning me that I didn't want to end the practice he had been a party to for more than ten years.

The same special treatment was afforded to antique dealers and resale shop owners. That meant all the good merchandise never saw the light of the sales floor. By eliminating the backroom, back-door policy, sales automatically increased. I found out months later that the reason my position had been open in the first place was because the previous manager had helped himself to that merchandise, as well. He and his girlfriend owned a resale shop, and he was in direct competition with Nonprofit, Inc. It was a conflict of interest that amounted to stealing from the handicapped since the merchandise he used to stock his store was the best that came through the donation system, and he didn't always pay for it.

As an aside - my assistant manager Bob was none to happy with the changes I'd made. He was even less happy with the fact that a black guy had been hired to replace his old boss. Within a few months Bob would pay someone $1800.00 to kill me. I found out the next day from his wife and sister-in-law who were with him at the time of the solicitation. Since money actually changed hands, I'd endured a few frightening days wondering how serious the situation was. The plot, it turned out, was nothing more than some guy in a bar taking advantage of Bob's drunken state - agreeing to do the deed in order to relieve him of the money Bob waved in the air for all in attendance to see, as he loudly made his desire to end my life known.

The details of how it all played out is another story that may be worth telling some day.

By the end of that year, those sales increases amounted to over a hundred thousand dollars in revenue. Ergo, my promotion to manage both stores. When I took over the main store location, I instituted the same policies. The difference there was that the quality merchandise, antiques, and other valuables, like jewelry, were going out the front door at discounted prices to special customers. The results were the same.

It was the early eighties. The economy was in the toilet, and the policies of a new conservative Reagan administration were taking their toll on funding for government programs that helped organizations like Nonprofit, Inc. Improvement of our own revenue through retail operations was essential just to keep us from losing ground.

I was in the right place at the right time, I would say. And when the organization decided they needed to open a third store, I was promoted a second time to the sales manager position. The first item on the agenda: promote Sandy, the assistant manager at the main store, to the store manager position and then hire her replacement as assistant manager.

The standard procedure for interviewing management at all levels was a minimum three-person panel. The panel for Sandy's replacement consisted of Sandy, Scott, and me. The best candidate for the job walked through the door in our third round of interviews. However, one of his answers to an interview question would sink his chances for the job. Sandy asked, "What do you think the most important part of your job would be?" His answer: "My job is to know your job so when you are on vacation or out of the building for any reason, I run the store the way you want it run."

Sandy and I thought this was a great response. Indeed, that was the most important part of his job. It not only served Sandy, it served the organization, ensuring there was consistency. By learning and understanding the store manager's job, he could be promoted when we expanded further.

Scott wasn't as impressed. Sandy and I were ready to make a job offer. Scott, as the top authority, put that notion to rest. He didn't like the way the candidate answered that question and actually pointed to it as a teaching moment for both Sandy and me. "He's too good," Scott said. "He's too experienced, and he's too ambitious. First, he's going to learn your job, Sandy, and then he's going to get your job. Then, Brian, he's going to learn your job and get your job. Then he'll be after my job, and I'm not going to let that happen."

And there it was—the first time I witnessed a job applicant rejected out of fear that he would be competition. At that moment, I cursed Scott. And I cursed the guy who'd hired me, Gary, because he'd gone and gotten himself promoted, and now I was stuck reporting to Scott.

Gary invited excellence, openness, and welcomed new employees into the organization. It was the reason he'd gone outside the company to fill the store manager position in the first place. He wanted someone who knew more about retail than he did. He wanted someone who hadn't learned everything they knew from the Nonprofit, Inc. model. He wanted innovation and change, "to shake things up," he would say. Now, I had this guy who feared competition and invited mediocrity.

Although I'd coached a few job applicants prior to going to work at Nonprofit, Inc., it had never been to overcome the fear-of-competition syndrome Scott offered as a teaching moment. His refusal to consider the possibility of hiring someone who was a top-grade forced me to coach all job applicants going forward.

The question that derailed the candidacy of that first applicant to whom Scott was afraid of losing his job was part of a standard script. When it came up again, along with any other questions that would provide a sense of a candidate's ambition at any level, I instructed the job applicant to give answers that met Scott's "less than" criteria.

The "hire people who are less qualified, even mediocre" mindset has grown exponentially over the years. I began noticing it more and more during my staffing company days from 1988 to 1996. During those years as a headhunter, the pattern emerged so often and at so many different client companies, my staff and I mused that there must be something in the water that was turning people stupid. Ron, my vice president of sales, offered the theory that it was the Russians. "The Chernobyl nuclear disaster was planned. They knew the jet stream would carry that nuclear fallout to our shores and get it into the water system."

I don't recall it being pervasive when I went to work at FSfoods in 1996, except when it came to using overqualification as an excuse to reject women or minority job applicants. To the best of my memory, it didn't really stand out much as something that came up on a regular basis again until I went to work at Kprints in 2000.

These days, unfair elimination isn't in the cards just because you are a woman, a minority, or too old. Growing economic uncertainty has made it more commonplace for the fear of competition.

To be certain, discriminatory bias is still rampant and is the overwhelming reason for job seekers to be treated unfairly. But fear of anyone who might compete for the next job or promotion has established a greater foothold in the mindset of hiring managers, and that affects everyone. This includes white males under forty who have traditionally been in the sweet spot as honorary members of the good old boys club. They are at risk if they are too smart, too successful, too competitive, or too ambitious.

The candidate that Scott refused to allow me to hire all those years ago was a white male. These days, someone may have a perfect work record but he or she can and are affected by some of the same strategies used to disguise discriminatory bias, unfairly weeding out the top-grade candidates, as well.

Proof of this growing phenomenon was provided in an April 17, 2011 *Newsweek* article with the title "The Beached White Male." It depicted the Ivy League-educated—who usually survive recessions—as "not only being on their knees but flat on their faces, perhaps permanently."

A recent survey of hiring managers also bears this out. It showed that over 94 percent of those questioned would prefer to hire someone they determined had the "right attitude but no skills, as opposed to someone who "ticked off every box of the qualifications but whose attitude wasn't quite right." The "attitude thing" is nothing more than code for managers to justify not hiring the most qualified due to that fear of hiring someone who might end up being competition for them.

One of the ironies of this aspect of the shifting hiring process is that it affects white males more than any other group, since they dominate the corporate culture. The other irony is that this "overqualified thing" has been the primary excuse hiring managers use to disguise discrimination, most notably against African Americans.

It's part of that cultural divide that goes back to slavery. Slaves weren't allowed to learn to read out of fear that they would smarten up, reading about freedoms and learning how to use maps and directions, all of which would either put in their minds the idea of escape and/or the means to be successful if they tried.

In modern society, keeping black people down (in their place) has meant keeping them beneath the authority or thumb of whites. This has translated into not hiring anyone who might show or demonstrate the ability to advance to a level where they would, in fact, have authority over white people. The same can be said for women and other minorities who've shown similar abilities. This strategy used by good old boys to cover up their discriminatory bias now threatens some of those same good old boys as much as it does the protected class.

The concept of hiring less-qualified, noncompetitive individuals became more prominent in those early days of my employment at Kprints, particularly after the economic downturn that occurred immediately following the events of 9/11. I mentioned in an earlier chapter how Liz, despite her superior abilities, lost out on a promotion to a white male who not only didn't measure up from a performance standard, he did not hold the required college education. The difference? Liz was a strong-minded, competent female and thus a threat.

At Uniforms, when my responsibilities expanded from two to three regions in late 2008, it was hard to distinguish what was really at play in the Gulf Coast. The director of sales for that region wasn't shy about eliminating what he described as overqualified job applicants for positions of territory sales reps or sales management.

Although he specifically stated he was rejecting one candidate for a district manager position because of age, the other decisions he made, and his general strategy of supporting the hiring of individuals who either had very little experience in sales or sales management, were more a sign of his fear of competition than illegal discriminatory bias.

Two human resource representatives for the region attributed all of the above not only to his hiring decision but those of managers throughout the region.

After twenty-one top-grade candidates failed to meet what he described as a "fit," I was at my wits' end. A job search that should have taken weeks turned into six months. The idea that I wasn't able to match his needs with twenty-one candidates said something, but I wasn't sure what.

One of the early candidates, I found out later from the local HR representative who'd interviewed her in person, was African American. Adam, the director of sales rejected her because, in his words, she was "too fragile" for Uniforms' rough – industrial environment. "She is used to a cleaner, more refined retail environment" like that of her most recent employer, AT&T, he said. "She would be shocked by our less than sophisticated branch locations," which he described as rough and dirty.

Another attempt to match his definition of "fit" had me soliciting the assistance of an outside headhunter. Her marching orders were to seek out job applicants from companies and environments where we'd hired from before. "They can't have made more money than our job pays," I instructed her. "They have to have been with the same company for more than five years," I told her, then listed every other reason Adam had used to disqualify other applicants, such as they weren't local and therefore wouldn't know the territory, they weren't service-oriented, and they didn't have the right personality.

She found a candidate with eight years of sales management experience with a company called Shred-It. Other general managers and directors of sales were keen on job candidates from this company. The business scheme and environment, I was told, were very similar to those at Uniforms. By that standard, everything was right with this candidate. Short of a personality conflict—the one excuse hard to overcome, whether it's a true concern or just pretext—this was a slam-dunk match, even for Adam, since one of his current sales managers had come from Shred-It.

The reason given for rejecting this candidate wasn't that clash of personality. In fact, all previous excuses for rejecting job applicants had been addressed. So I was surprised—no, flabbergasted—when the excuse was that the candidate had worked for a Shred-It franchise instead of the corporate organization. Adam said, "He won't be able to adjust to a larger corporate environment."

It's worth noting that this candidate was African American and over fifty, and I could easily surmise, based on the lack of minorities in management roles at Uniforms, that those were the reasons he wasn't allowed in. However, to the best of my knowledge, the majority of applicants rejected were white males. So, when it came to fear of competition, Adam and others like him were equal-opportunity offenders.

That brings me back to the whole fear of competition thing. To figure out what was really going on, I decided to conduct a test. I asked the recruiter to contact a candidate I had rejected based on what I'd seen on his resume. He lived in Dallas instead of south Texas, where the position was. There was a history of job-hopping; he'd worked for three different companies in six years. He'd only held a sales management position for two of those years and had taken a step back into sales by the time I'd found his information. The attributes I wanted to test were his underqualification in a management role and that he was under forty years of age, had an unstable work history, and was a white male.

In case you haven't guessed already, yes, he's the candidate Adam had wanted to hire. The reasons other candidates were rejected did not apply to this candidate, most notably the unstable work history, the undisputable proof that he had already failed in a management role, and his residence outside the job territory.

I provided Liz with a spreadsheet detailing all the candidates, their backgrounds, and the reasons they were rejected and offered my opinion that the whole of the information pointed to Adam's motivation being all of the above. Depending on the candidate, race, gender, and age discrimination played a role in his decision-making. However, fear of competition played just as much a role. White men and women with the solid experience that would allow them to hit the ground running were rejected in favor of this candidate, who would, at best, reach a level of competency that might allow him to survive, but there was no way he was going to shine in a way that would make him a threat to Adam.

It was my opinion, based on considerable comparison of facts, that just one aspect of the many ways pretext and double standards are used to eliminate job applicants unfairly contributed to what was already a quantifiably mediocre, if not incompetent, management core. However, with people like Adam making the decisions, it wasn't a leap. Given the opportunity, weak people will hire weaker people. Fearful people hire based on fear, biased people hire based on bias. And it's less likely that the standard will be broken unless it is forced.

I refer to the tactic of hiring less than qualified candidates as a plague because of the other similar incidents that occurred during my employment. For example, in Waterbury, Connecticut, we advertised for college grads to fill a management trainee position. The broader understanding of "college grad," without specifying "recent college grad," provided cover if anyone made the accusation that there was intent of only hiring young people for the opening. After all, college grad could mean anyone with a college degree, regardless of how old they were. You would never know that behind the scenes the company was pushing the qualification of youth. To them, it meant recent college grad, as in fresh out of school, with little or no experience.

It is only by looking at the records of those disqualified compared to those who were hired that this comes to light.

Individuals above the age of forty were never considered, despite the fact that their track record of a strong work ethic offered proof that they would be an asset to the company. Equally, others who didn't fall into that forty threshold where age discrimination law begins but who had years of quantifiable experience were passed over as well.

At that same location, there was also an open human resource generalist position.

The regional vice president was pushing the idea of only filling the management trainee position and allowing that person, a rookie out of college, to take on the HR generalist duties as well. He tried to sell it as part of the overall development of the manager trainee.

As Liz—who told me about the heated exchange between herself, the VP, and Jennie, the senior executive of human resources—put it, "It's pretty clear he just wants to hire some rookie he can control and who will be more beholden to operations then HR."

In the Southern region, the candidate who was finally hired for the director of sales position was not the most qualified of the applicants. The highest level position he'd held was district sales manager. This would be a promotion from direct management of territory salespeople to direct management of district managers who managed those salespeople. Others involved in the hunt had actually held the director position and above in the past. But the candidate was, as the VP described, "young and a go-getter."

With this kind of thinking, anyone could see how it was that this company struggled to maintain the momentum of year after year revenue growth.

A strong economy raises all boats, even those of the mediocre and incompetent. It's when times are tough, like the economic downturn that began shortly thereafter, that separates the good from the bad. Uniforms took a hit to the tune of more than two hundred million in annual revenue when the economy turned south while others in the industry were holding steady or improving. I believe a cultural tendency, because of fear of competition by rank-and-file middle management, to avoid hiring the most qualified contributed to the negative growth.

Anyone in business who reads this will want to say, "Not me!" And maybe it's not them, but there is risk in not considering the possibility.

Consider a study by Edward Fulton Denison published in 1985, *Trends of American Economic Growth, 1929–1982* , which included this statement: "A sizable body of informed opinion holds that performance of American management, as it relates to productivity, has deteriorated badly since 1973."

CHAPTER 24

Diversity Central

Comedian, actor, author, and host of *The Daily Show*, Jon Stewart, garners hero status. Although I have to confess that I know little of his true character beyond what is billed as a "fake news show with the best fucking news team ever," I dare say the glimpse he offers the public is much more telling than, maybe, even he would like to acknowledge.

The nightly delivery of information that brings us face to face with the absurdity of social and political events makes his so-called fake news more real and thought-provoking than what we might find on the "real" news shows.

As entertaining his delivery, as enlightening his program's content, Stewart's hero status is earned from the subtle message that comes from observing the makeup of the cast and crew who bring us this groundbreaking show.

Samantha Bee since 2001; Wyatt Cynac, 2008; Jason Jones, 2004; Assif Manvi, 2006; Olivia Munn, 2010; Al Madrigal, 2011; John Oliver, 2006; Lewis Black, 1996; Larry Wilmore, 2006; John Hodgeman, 2006; Kristen Schaal, 2008—along with Stewart, these are the people whose diverse faces represent *The Daily Show*.

I have some questions for Jon Stewart. They are the same questions every CEO and top executive in any company should be asking. How did you do it? How have you been able to maintain it year after year? No, I'm not talking about the top ratings and overall success. I'm talking about the diversity. How is it *The Daily Show* has been able to achieve what most corporations have not?

At least two Jews and African Americans; women; Muslim, Hispanic, and white guys; old white guys; an Asian; Canadians; and an Englishman—and that's just in front of the camera. Behind the scenes, from producers and writers to technicians, the cultural representation is complete. I submit that *The Daily Show* is an example of how easy it is for a corporation to achieve diversity.

Now, maybe it isn't easy. Maybe it is painstakingly difficult. The main point here is that Stewart does it.

I also submit that if Jon Stewart can achieve this in a difficult industry like entertainment—where top talent is difficult to come by regardless of what they look like or where they come from—the rest of corporate America, with countless numbers of people from all walks of life who have the prerequisite education, training, and experience, should be able to do it without difficulty.

History tells us that there are companies like Shoney's restaurants and FSfoods that were doomed to cultures of discrimination from the date their founders opened the doors. Others, like Darden Restaurants, started out with diversity and maintained it. Others still, despite claims of efforts, failed, with the exception of those that took extraordinary actions on their own or were forced by legal decree.

So far, I have highlighted two CEOs—Jacobson at Denny's and Roberts at RadioShack—who not only did it right but called out corporate America's lack of progress in this area. I would be remiss if I didn't also point out that both these companies have been engaged in lawsuits over discrimination since.

In September 2010, a lawsuit filed by the U.S. Equal Employment Opportunity Commission alleged that RadioShack Corp. discriminated against a fifty-five-year-old employee because of his age and retaliated against him when he complained. In the lawsuit, the employee claimed that the electronics supplier assigned a younger regional manager to supervise him in 2007. That manager put the plaintiff on two performance improvement plans, despite what the lawsuit said was a twenty-five-year, spotless performance record. When the employee complained to human resources, he was terminated, according to the lawsuit.

Another news story told us about continued problems at Denny's. On September 15, 2007, a federal jury awarded $600,000 in damages to a family that sued the Denny's restaurant chain for racial discrimination. Attorneys for the family said a white waiter deliberately ignored them and used racial slurs during a meal at a Denny's restaurant in the St. Louis suburb of Fairview Heights. The waiter later was fired. Each of fifteen family members was awarded

$5,000 in compensatory damages and $35,000 in punitive in U.S. District Court in East St. Louis, Illinois.

Before this book went to print, allegations of systemic discrimination against African Americans at one of Darden's Restaurant chains (the Capitol Grille) was reported in The Huffington Post on February 6, 2012.

Even *The Daily Show*, despite its efforts, has detractors when it comes to diversity in the female category. A blogger at www.Jezebel.com put it like this:

"*The Daily Show* is many things: progressive darling, alleged news source for America's youth, righteous media critique. And it's also a boys' club where women's contributions are often ignored and dismissed.

If Olivia Munn, the former videogame show host introduced to *Daily Show* viewers three weeks ago, survives her tryout, she'll be the first new female correspondent on the show in seven years. With the notable exception of Samantha Bee, who's been on since 2001, female correspondents have been a short-lived phenomenon. As fiercely liberal and sharp-eyed an observer as Jon Stewart can be, getting women on the air may be his major blind spot."

In response, the women who work there provided a view—through an open letter on the program's website, www.thedailyshow.com —that is in line with the evidence of wholesale diversity and inclusion:

"Dear People Who Don't Work Here,

Recently, certain media outlets have attempted to tell us what it's like to be a woman at *The Daily Show* with Jon Stewart. We must admit it is entertaining to be the subjects of such a vivid and dramatic narrative. However, while rampant sexism at a well-respected show makes for a great story, we want to make something very clear: the place you may have read about is not our office.

The Daily Show isn't a place where women quietly suffer on the sidelines as barely tolerated tokens. On the contrary: just like the men here, we're indispensable. We generate a significant portion of the show's creative content and the fact is, it wouldn't be the show that you love without us.

So, who are the women of *The Daily Show*?

If you think the only women who help create this show are a couple of female writers and correspondents, you're dismissing the vast majority of us. Actually, we make up 40 percent of the staff, and we're not all shoved into the party-planning department (although we do run that, and we throw some kick-ass parties). We are co-executive producers, supervising producers, senior producers, segment producers, coordinating field producers, associate producers, editors, writers, correspondents, talent coordinators, production coordinators, researchers, makeup artists, the entire accounting and audience departments, production assistants, crew members, and much more. We were each hired because of our creative ability, our intelligence, and above all, our ability to work our asses off to make a great show......"

The Letter goes on and essentially demolishes any notion that Job Stewart and the Daily Show is discriminatory or a good old boys club, ending with this statement:

"The truth is, when it comes down to it, The Daily Show isn't a boy's club or a girl's club, it's a family—a highly functioning if sometimes dysfunctional family. And we're not thinking about how to maximize our gender roles in the workplace on a daily basis. We're thinking about how to punch up a joke about Glenn Beck's latest diatribe, where to find a Michael Steele puppet on an hour's notice, which chocolate looks most like an oil spill, and how to get a gospel choir to sing the immortal words, "Go f@#k yourself!"

Blog posts that cling to the narrative about sexism at *The Daily Show* are quick to dismiss the open letter; One mused: "As current employees, what else would they say?"

I submit they didn't have to say anything at all. They could have allowed the boys-club stories to advance or die in the media through their own momentum based on interest of the public. The significance of the women's collective response comes from comparison to how many times we have seen others defend the companies they worked for when charges of discriminatory culture were made. The challenge is to find someone other than a company representative who was hired to be the company mouthpiece.

My point is that there is evidence that there is a natural tendency by Jon Stewart to want inclusion and diversity, as well as a concerted effort to ensure it. There is also evidence that it has been extremely successful. Whether one looks at *The Daily Show* or companies like Denny's, RadioShack, or Darden Restaurants, they all demonstrate that the excuses and roadblocks to achieving diversity cited by hiring managers and the companies themselves are just that—excuses.

Every company can—by decree of the CEO, with follow-through by managers and support through policies and systems of accountability—achieve the inclusion and diversity demonstrated by *The Daily Show*.

By virtue of the-fact that the corporate landscape generally has not achieved it, coupled with my own experience as a corporate insider, there is ample evidence that the failure is purposeful.

CHAPTER 25

Solutions

In 1996, my proposal to the president of FSfoods to establish a system of checks and balances, in which an impartial panel would review the hiring and rejection decisions by hiring managers, was not an idea I originated. Neither was the idea of a position profile based solely on specific job duties. In fact, some forms of these concepts have been in the corporate domain for decades. The only difference is that they weren't utilized to weed out discriminatory hiring practices.

Oversight has been a constant in corporate America. Supervisors routinely interview candidates that their subordinates want to hire. Panel interviews, like the example at Nonprofit, Inc., are designed to gain consensus on qualifications of applicants. And, as I pointed out with the information I provided with the panel interviews at Kprints, there are processes in place in which, by mere participation of the proper authority figure, hiring managers are forced to not only hire the most qualified but to keep their discriminatory bias in check.

My FSfoods suggestion of voluntary oversight by an independent panel arose from the decrees that companies like Denny's, Coke, and Texaco agreed to in the wake of their historic discrimination lawsuits and settlements.

Kenneth Labich, wrote the following in his follow-up story for *Money* magazine in September 1999, about the success of the Coke diversity initiative.

"By agreeing to submit their employment practices to outside scrutiny, Coke did reclaim a position as one of the best when it comes to diversity, as did Denny's restaurants and Texaco.

The Texaco Task Force on Equality and Fairness has submitted annual reports to the court that show that the safeguards implemented there have been wildly successful. So much so, reporter Labich, who has followed the story from the beginning wrote, "So, here's a shocker: Texaco, still perceived by many as a chamber of horrors for minorities, is in the midst of a remarkable transformation, one that just may turn the company into a bastion of equal opportunity for people of color. In time, it may even become a model for any corporation that wants to learn how to become more hospitable to employees of all races."

Labich offered this information as proof:

"Just how far has Texaco come? Here are a few numbers worth noting: Last year minorities accounted for nearly four in ten new hires at Texaco and more than 20 percent of promotions. During the first six months of 1999, minorities accounted for 44 percent of new hires and 22 percent of promotions. In 1996, company officials vowed to spend at least $1 billion with minority- and women-owned vendors—or about 15 percent of overall spending—before 2001."

Here's another telling note highlighted by Labich: "Company officials were feeling good enough about themselves earlier this year to apply for inclusion in Fortune's 1999 list of America's 50 Best Companies for Asians, Blacks, and Hispanics (July 19). Texaco didn't make the cut, but the very fact the firm aspired to make the list (and actually believed it had a chance) says plenty about how some folks there are feeling about themselves these days on matters of race. And at least one diversity expert says their new attitude may indeed be warranted. "I have never seen a company be so creative and so dedicated to change," says Weldon Latham, a senior partner at the Washington, D.C., law firm Shaw Pittman and a prominent racial-harassment litigator. "They are absolutely a model for how to approach one of the biggest problems facing this country."

The quick success of these and other companies show the path for all corporations to eliminate the ugly, corrupt cultures of discrimination.

I dare say that if FSfoods had voluntarily initiated even the limited oversight I suggested in 1996, they would have accomplished the same thing and wouldn't have faced a company-wide investigation of their hiring practices by the EEOC in 2011.

Unfortunately, voluntary adoption of "the model," which has proven to have the desired effect of dramatically transforming corporate America across the landscape into bastions of diversity and inclusion, has not occurred.

This fact is another pillar in the argument that corporate America isn't interested in anything but maintaining the status quo. It's also evidence to bolster the argument that government—in its role as protector of individual rights, freedom, and civil liberties—has an obligation to establish regulations that will force companies to adopt this oversight model.

Equally, it is government's responsibility and within government's power to strengthen discrimination laws ensuring that companies don't continue to have the advantage of unlimited funds to fight individuals who don't have such funds, as well as strengthen penalties against individuals within the corporate system who perpetrate discrimination.

The solution begins with attacking the problem at the source by expanding existing laws that determine criminality related to individual acts of discrimination. As it stands today, criminality is limited to federally protected activities where the civil rights violation includes willful injury, intimidation, or interference with any person, or an attempt to do so, by force or threat of force. The key words—by force or threat of force—virtually dictate that violence has to be involved in order for it to be criminal.

The first case of criminal violation and prosecution occurred in Philadelphia, Mississippi, with the murders of civil rights workers, James Chaney, Andrew Goodman, and Michael Schwerner. A state jury acquitted accused KKK members of murder. The federal government charged them with civil rights violations. They went to jail.

There was the infamous case of the police officers who viciously beat Rodney King in 1992, which also resulted in jail time for those officers under the Civil Rights Act. There have been many others, including the most recent indictment of a New York City police officer on charges of false arrest, malicious prosecution, and violent extortion, was reported by CBS news on Oct. 17, 2011.

Individuals who discriminate should also face penalty of jail time, as well as personal obligation for monetary restitution. This is not a leap, considering the far-reaching negative implications on an individual's constitutional right to pursue happiness and the significance a job, and thus financial advancement, plays in relation to the pursuit of happiness. The deprivation of an individual's right to work is equally as offensive and damaging as acts of violence. The long-term implications are even more so when considering the statistics that suggest shortened lifespan for minorities and women who, because of lack of opportunity in the workplace, are left without financial means to maintain health care.

Second step: apply RICO-type statutes to corporations. In 1989, the Justice Department brought a racketeering case against the International Brotherhood of Teamsters (IBT), saying that it was a "wholly owned subsidiary of organized crime." Since 1992, an independent review board has overseen Teamster elections.

I submit that while the money Coke, Texaco, and Denny's paid out reached into the tens and hundreds of millions, it was nothing when considering their revenue and profits and therefore it's not a deterrent. I submit that it was the public scrutiny that ultimately forced them to comply with the law. However, imagine if the penalty had been in the billions. Imagine if they'd lost control under receivership. These are the kinds of far-reaching penalties that will deter individuals and companies from violating civil rights.

That said, our political and social climate all but dictate that no such transformation will take place anytime soon. If anything, the evidence suggests that with the influence of corporate America on the political landscape—including the Supreme Court decision classifying corporations as people and thereby allowing unlimited corporate funds into our political process—the opposite is more likely. This means real people will continue to be at a disadvantage.

As our system operates today, beyond the disadvantage of not having the financial wherewithal to pursue a discrimination case when there is clear-cut evidence, laws are easily manipulated. Interpretations of the threshold required to prove discrimination is skewed in an employer's favor.

Without forced compliance through regulation, even as the EEOC racks up wins against corporations, hiring managers and corporations have unparalleled advantages.

Since the enactment of civil rights and related equal employment laws, beyond the secret codes, double standards, and pretext has been the preferred method for most managers and companies.

This is how it works. Job candidates A and B both held three jobs in ten years, ample reason for some to label them job-hoppers and therefore not a fit. However, only candidate A is given that label and rejected for the job. Candidate B gets the benefit of a doubt—and the job. The difference? Candidate A is a minority or a female or over forty, or maybe candidate A disclosed a disability, religion, or marital status. Candidate B is a white male in his thirties. The same double-standard trick can be applied to any job applicant, at any time, using any one of the generally accepted criteria within any company.

Without regulations mandating the uniformity of qualification standards and the independent oversight boards to ensure those standards are adhered to, hiring managers and companies will continue to succeed in maintaining the status quo. Even as the EEOC racks up wins, companies will adapt and refine the one area of the recruiting and interviewing process that will continue to wreak havoc on the prospects of accountability at every level. Companies know that the law, as it stands today, is in their favor as long as they maintain loose standards and related interpretation of qualifications. It maintains the deceptive practice of double standards and pretext. They know that, without meeting some specific definition established by law, the argument for discrimination by arguing pretext is difficult to prove.

Here's a case illustrating that. Millbrook v. IBP, Inc. was a lawsuit involving a white male candidate and an African American. The African American alleged that he was discriminated against despite having better qualifications than the white applicant who was hired. The Seventh Circuit Court of Appeals considered this set of facts. The plaintiff argued that the employer's explanation for its failure to hire him was a mere pretext. However, the court noted that the burden of proving such motive is high, saying that "'pretext' means a lie. Specifically a phony reason for some action…it means something worse than a business error; 'pretext' means deceit used to cover one's tracks."

In this case, the plaintiff asserted that certain subjective factors were used in the selection process. The court noted that even if the employer used subjective hiring criteria in its decision-making, this does not necessarily give rise to a Title 7 claim. The plaintiff must prove that these factors served as a "mask for discrimination." The plaintiff also argued that he was more qualified to hold the position than the winning candidate. While the court noted that both candidates appeared to be qualified, the plaintiff must be able to demonstrate that his resume was so far superior to the others that there can be no reasonable dispute (absent some evidence of intentional discrimination by the employer).

Without regulation or oversight, the tactic of using double standards and pretext is how hiring managers get away with discrimination, and it's the maintenance of lack of qualifications standards that will allow corporations to deny and litigate, using their lopsided advantage of money and power.

One way to level the playing field is for the government to include in regulations the requirement that job applicants who are rejected be provided a copy of the qualifications of the individual who was hired in their place. This can be done without a breach of privacy for that individual.

That said, it also has to be acknowledged that, although there are signs (Occupy Wall Street) that individuals are beginning to wake up and demand that government right wrongs within the system, the political and social climate is at a crossroads. The rise of the Tea Party offers a view that there is just as much a chance that there will be less government intervention.

The Supreme Court decision declaring "corporations are people" adds to the power and influence of corporations in government to thwart any effort to establish new regulations, and there are those who are fighting to eliminate individuals' protections.

In either case, whatever the outcome of the current battle, in the interim individuals are by and large left to their own devices. That, again, begs the question—what are we willing to do?

The answer—short of someone determining that they are going to take their chances with the system, short of having the luck of getting a job with the likes of Jon Stewart's *Daily Show* or companies like Coke and Texaco that have eliminated systemic discrimination—brings us back to the concept of anything goes.

CHAPTER 26

Stealing Jobs

With or without the benefit of an insider like me who is willing to run interference for a job applicant, the solution to beating the unfair system is available.

The basis for adopting the solution is in taking on the posture that, as a job seeker, as an individual, we have an equal right to the strategies and rules of corporations.

Society allows for certain kind of lies. We have even given it a name, "little white lies." However, in an advertisement from a background check company, they argue that when it comes to the application process employers should consider that even little white lies are a sign of questionable honesty and integrity of a potential employee.

The background check company, in their efforts to demonize job applicants in order to increase the value of and necessity for their services, goes as far as to describe any misrepresentation by a job applicant as an attempt to "steal their way to the head of the line," in essence, steal a job.

The example they provide to explain "stealing a job" has to do with age. They write: "Another resume lie to look for is the omission of information, such as the year they earned a degree or taking large portions out of their work history to appear more youthful." The advertisement in the form of an article goes on to say: "Although this may seem like a minor offense, honesty is something most hiring managers are looking for, and it doesn't say much about an applicant who lies."

To that we should all be asking in a loud voice, "Really?"

Age discrimination is on the rise. Job applicants are routinely weeded out because of their age during the resume review process. This is a fact! There is no law or requirement that dates of graduation are necessary. Beyond that, job seekers are advised to limit their resume information to one or two pages. Many an executive has been quoted as saying he or she won't even look at a resume that is more than one page. This reality of what actually occurs in the job market dictates that job applicants reduce their information to that which is relevant to the job they are applying for. Yet, job seekers, according to this background check company, are now to be judged as having questionable integrity simply because they leave out information that is irrelevant, isn't necessary, isn't required, and has the potential to hurt their chances! Really?

By those standards, any company, any hiring manager, anywhere is free to use whatever benchmark they wish to determine the honesty and integrity of a job applicant and, thus, the applicant's employability.

This is how totally lopsided and, therefore, ridiculous the entire job search game is. And believe me, it is a game. While one person might perceive a legitimate reason not to disclose certain information, another can perceive that failure to disclose that information is a viable reason to determine employability.

My point is the rules are made up by who knows who, for what reason, influenced by whomever, for whatever reason, often having no applicability to law or reason.

My advice to job seekers is that, with few exceptions, you have as much right to make up your own rules of how you present your qualifications to potential employers as they have. As a company assumes a right to inflate, even lie, about how wonderful their job and corporate culture are—despite what might be hiding behind closed doors, despite what might be lurking in legal responses to EEOC complaints or a courtroom drama—you have the same right.

FSfoods didn't disclose their discriminatory history until after I accepted the job. They didn't tell job applicants that the reason they wanted to conduct a home visit as part of the interview was to find out if they were really married or what their personal habits were. Explaining this policy, one general manager told me how he and others lied to job applicants. He told them the reason for the home visit was to sit down with an applicant and his spouse to review the health insurance and other benefits because of their complexity. Huh!

Shoney's didn't inform Roberts of their discriminatory past before he accepted the CEO job. Uniforms doesn't tell job applicants for route sales jobs that they have been sued for wage violations. They don't disclose they were sued for environmental contamination in two states or that they paid out over $2 million to settle the charges over those environmental violations. No one told job applicants at one of their Florida locations that one of their managers was a convicted child sex offender.

At the time Uniforms replied to my EEOC complaint, it wasn't to their advantage to disclose that a number of other HR people had also filed complaints or that they were in the middle of litigation over discrimination because of a workers' compensation claim. They left out the important fact that Shitty, the instigator of the retaliation against me, had been investigated by the company for similar conduct. Instead, they highlighted all the positive things they do to ensure discrimination doesn't occur and is dealt with when it does.

We, as individuals, have as much right to present our information in whatever manner, to whatever extent, we choose. We have a right to disclose or withhold information. Especially if doing so protects us from being weeded out by standards based on consideration of factors that are violation of law.

My advice to job applicants is to protect yourselves as companies protect themselves.

We know companies discriminate based on age, sex, race, disability, national origin, and religion. We know your lifestyle—including married with children, divorced with children, single parent, questionable credit—are all illegal considerations employers have based decisions on. We also know they will discriminate against you if you are unemployed.

Everything an employer does—from the first step of reviewing a resume to the application, interview questions, integrity tests, psychological assessments, and background check—is designed to find out as much about you as they can. The more information you give them, the easier it is to weed you out.

Employers want the perfect candidate. The definition of perfect is subject to interpretation by anyone within the company structure.

My advice? Be the perfect candidate, starting with your resume and application.

Make it hard for them to weed you out. The only way to do that is to be the perfect candidate. Because here's the thing: even the perfect candidate, when it comes to legal considerations like longevity on the job, job title, industry, duties, education, has less than a 50 percent chance of getting the job if that candidate is a woman, over forty, or a minority. Job applicants, depending on who they are, what they look like, even how they talk, are automatically at a disadvantage because of negative-bias stereotypes.

Consider this: Princeton sociologist Devah Pager reported in the *American Journal of Sociology* that "white job applicants in Milwaukee with felony convictions were more likely to get job offers than equally qualified blacks with no criminal background." In this instance, it begs the question, does honesty really matter? What possible excuse could there be for choosing a white applicant with a felony conviction over a minority "with no criminal background"?

Consider what happened to Michael. He was one of the candidates for a district manager position that I presented to a panel interview at Kprints. He met the definition of perfect candidate. While some of the others had inconsequential baggage that could be exploited, he had none. In fact, his work record was spotless—the same company for fifteen years, steady advancement from store manager to district manager and then regional director. He was on par in responsibility with the regional VP who was passing judgment on him. However, his pay wasn't commensurate with his position. That gave us something to offer to entice him, as well as upward mobility. He was the embodiment of top-grade. Oh, yeah, and he was African American. And he was good-looking and spoke well. I'm not sure why that's always a relevant factor when considering black people but it was, and it is.

Michael aced every question, even the last one, which came out of left field and seemed irrelevant. "What did you get out of the master's degree program your company paid to put you through?" His answer was honest. If I had known they would use it to disqualify him or that they would even ask the question in the first place, I would have coached him on the answer ahead of time. "Not much," he said. "I'd already had five years of real-life marketing in my current position, so there really wasn't anything new." His employer paid for the degree program and that factor became the focus of the debrief. Words like "ungrateful: dotted the conversation, which ended with the panel rejecting him for the job.

Even if you are the perfect candidate in every reasonable, legal consideration, you are still at risk if there is a culture of discrimination.

My advice to job applicants is less is more. This means leave your baggage at home. It means only provide information that is relevant to the job you are applying for. It means eliminate anything that can be used against you. It also means make it as difficult as possible for them to weed you out. And, if by chance, you don't get the job and you suspect discrimination, the record of your perfect work history will serve you well if you decide to take legal action.

The only thing that matters is whether you have the experience required. That's why my advice to job applicants is don't lie about your experience. From my view, falsification of your actual experience, skills, and related ability to do a job will not serve you well. You may be able to fake it for a while, but eventually your lack of experience will show up and then your employer can legally fire you. You have no defense. Equally, it's important to note that falsification of information related to certain government or security-related positions is a crime. In some states, there are laws on the books that make it a misdemeanor to falsify higher education.

That said, until all other considerations are equally applied, everything else is fair game—and when you're applying for a job, it all matters.

Age matters. The law protecting individuals against age discrimination begins at age forty. Most of us are safe from this particularly disturbing discrimination until we hit our fifties. My advice is to eliminate anything on your resume that might give them a clue that you are older than forty years old. That means no dates for when you graduated. Only show ten to fifteen years of work history. If you have prior work experience that may be relevant for the job you are applying for, add a summary at the end with a general statement of skills and expertise. No dates, no titles, no anything else.

If they ask your age on a job application, lie.

Over-qualifications matter. I suggest there is no such thing as over-qualification. It really is just a way to hide discrimination. To avoid being categorized as overqualified, there has to be consideration of three elements of the information a job applicant provides— salary history, job title and duties.

Salary history: If a job applicant made more money from their last or current job, a hiring manager will, for a variety of reasons, be reluctant to make a job offer. If you want to be considered for that job, your best bet is to come up with a salary that is equal to or lower than the salary of the position you are applying for.

Job title: For example, a director of human resource title may weed you out if you are applying for an HR manager role. It's fair and reasonable to reduce your title to match the job.

Duties: The same rules apply to revenue you may be responsible for, number of people supervised, number of locations, and size of facility or territory.

Unemployment matters. No one has to show they are unemployed. Since job applicants are unfairly being disqualified simply for being unemployed, why would you?

You have two options. If you have been unemployed for less than six months, it's common to show your employment "to present" on your resume. The only thing left is to decide whether you are going to follow through on that statement or explain your current situation. My advice is to use someone you trust as a reference instead of giving them the actual company contact information. A friend, a spouse using her maiden name, anyone who is willing to give the dates of employment you want used. Or you can come clean during the interview, hoping your skills, experience, enthusiasm, and winning personality will overcome any concerns.

Your second option is to create your own company, giving yourself the job title you are applying for. It costs less than $50 to create a website. Again, you'll need someone to be your reference. The key here is to make sure you don't call yourself the boss or a consultant. Owning your own business is a negative for most people in corporate America. Will you be able to adapt to having to report to someone? Why are you looking to get out of that business? The HR people have already decided that it's because you weren't good enough to make the business work. In short, you are a failure.

Termination matters. Never, ever admit you were terminated. The chance of them finding out is minimal. Former employers are reluctant to give out that kind of information.

Credit history matters. Company rules and policies vary and they are changing. Credit history may or may not be relevant. Bottom line, if the company considers credit history, it is what it is. However, what job applicants have to watch out for is the individual manager, HR person, even a recruiter, they may be dealing with. These people have their own views on what poor credit history says about a job applicant. Too many job applicants have been compelled to divulge bad history up-front in an effort to explain it in terms they think will mitigate the effect once a background check is conducted. It doesn't. You are simply offering the red flag that will allow the company to eliminate you without the benefit of having demonstrated your skills or experience for the job.

Personal information matters. Politics, religion, marital status, family, social activities, sports—just don't. Any and all may be appealing or not. The fact is it gives the company way too much information about you. The only exceptions are those situations in which you know for a fact that the company looks at such information favorably. For example, many companies take positive note of community activities.

Before I get to the issue of criminal history, I need to reiterate a few things. First and foremost, as an example of my personal view of certain crimes, child molesters especially, but sex offenders of any kind should be put in jail for the rest of their lives. I am especially appalled at the fact that some child molesters are set free. I certainly don't want to work alongside them. I don't want to have to work with someone who committed any kind of violent crime, any more than I want to work with someone who hates black people. I agree with a company policy that weeds out such people within the parameters established by law. The fact that the policies are not applied equally to all job applicants is the reason I offer this advice on disclosure of criminal history.

Criminal background matters. It's a hard one. Back in the days before 9/11 and the Patriot Act, job applicants were less likely to get caught failing to disclose criminal convictions, depending on where the crimes had occurred and how far the company went in investigating such matters. What was certain was if you disclosed a felony or even a misdemeanor on a resume, you were weeded out— again, depending on what you looked like. Some companies only checked county records, some went statewide, and others conducted background checks in every municipality where you'd lived. So if you had a felony conviction for firing a weapon in Orange County, Florida—as was the case with Wayne—but you were applying for a job with a company in Kenosha County, Wisconsin, the only way the company would know about the felony is if you'd disclosed it on your application, or you'd disclosed that you'd lived or worked in Orange County, Florida.

Before 9/11, my advice to an applicant was not to disclose any kind of criminal record. I still offer the same advice today, although it needs to be understood that the chance of a company finding out is greater. But here's the thing. Depending on the efficiency of the process, undisclosed criminal history that shows up on a background check may be overlooked. There is also a chance it will not show up at all.

Because consideration of criminal background isn't applied equally, and just as often a minority will be bounced for a criminal conviction far less severe than that of a white male applicant, all job applicants are better off not disclosing the information up front. Chances are they will automatically be eliminated without consideration of whether the crime is relevant to the job.

Gaps in employment matter. This issue has the same negative connotation as being unemployed. The same rules apply. The gaps need to be filled in.

Job-hopping matters. It's a legitimate concern. It may or may not reflect instability of a job applicant, but a company has the right to determine whether they should invest time, money, and effort.

From a job applicant's point of view, if a company expects a history of longevity on the job then the prospective employee has a right to expect some assurance of job longevity from the company. Unfortunately, unless there is a specific contract of employment, no such assurance is forthcoming. Companies—on whim to meet any financial savings or purchase new equipment that may eliminate a job—are free to hire and fire as they choose. Indeed, companies have fought against unions and lobbied for the concept of right-to-work statutes at the state level. Beyond employers' lopsided expectations, there is often the question of whether change in jobs is more reflective of an industry or a company, rather than the stability of an individual. Over the past twenty years, downsizing, mergers, acquisitions, and outsourcing have been widespread and continuous, thus providing fuel for that argument. There is an argument that employers have no more right to expect an employee do anything more than work diligently for whatever period of time they are employed than an employee has of expecting to get nothing more than the wage agreed to for the work they have done.

That said, like many of the legal criteria (unrelated to discrimination), I may disagree with its use but I have faithfully weeded out job applicants in those corporate environments and situations where I believed the standards were applied equally to all candidates. It is only because longevity on the job and other criteria are applied unequally that I advise job applicants to eliminate jobs from their resumes and fill in the time with their own employment for a longer period and/or change the length of employment for any of the jobs. The latter works if the company you worked for went out of business or merged with another company.

While employers may be able to eliminate you from consideration or terminate your employment if you misrepresent your information, some of the advice they receive from attorneys is that it's not as cut and dry as it may seem.

Success in defending decisions to eliminate a job applicant or an employee because of false representations relies heavily on two factors.

First, the company has to demonstrate that they have acted consistently when they discover a lie, regardless of when they discover it. Second, the falsification has to be material to the duties of the job held or being applied for.

If you are qualified for the job, if you have the experience, nothing else should matter. If you've presented yourself as a perfect job applicant by eliminating anything that is detrimental, a company still doesn't make you the job offer, and you believe that you were discriminated against, even if the company is able to show a court that you misrepresented or left something out, it won't matter when deciding the case.

I said it earlier in the book, but it is worth repeating. The question I ask is this: would you rather tell the truth and never have a chance at the job at all—not even an interview—or risk being found out later, but at least have a chance?

Since every individuals situation is different, the only other advice that can be universally applied and therefore worth mentioning, is resume formatting. Despite arguments that there are no differences in resume formats, there are. One type of format will raise suspicion. A chronological resume provides the kind of information in a format that the majority of employers expect. Job titles, dates, of employment, job duties and accomplishments. A functional resume highlights job duties and accomplishments without showing dates of employment and companies worked for. It is an automatic assumption that users of the functional resume are trying to hide something—job-hopping, gaps in employment, unemployment, age.

Unless a job applicant knows specifically that an employer wants to see experience in that format, don't use it, ever. It's a one-way ticket to the round file or delete button.

With the chronological resume, there is still opportunity to highlight skills and accomplishments before they get to work history. You can still include an objective as long as it is short and to the point. The most important thing is to make sure they get to your actual work history quickly, no later than a third of the page down.

From my view, if a job applicant claims experience they do not have, the background-check company is right, he or she is attempting to steal a job. However, that is the only instance in which the theft allegation can be made.

The fact is that hiring managers and companies, through the various tactics they utilize to weed out qualified job applicants, are the ones who actually steal jobs.

CHAPTER 27

The Last Word

Why bother speaking up and challenging the system when it always ends up negatively for you? If your conscience won't allow you to go along, why not just work underground? At least that way you keep a job and advance.

These are the questions and comments that come from family, friends, and acquaintances who have come to know the trials and tribulations of my work.

The issue comes up often. Each time it's a new chance for them to convince me to give up and just go along. For my part, I have resorted to glib responses; their prodding provides the opportunity to channel the phrase attributed to Senator Robert F. Kennedy: "If not now, when? If not me, who?"

Of course, the answer is not as simple as that, and indeed there is no one answer.

Here's the thing. Working underground coaching job applicants is good for protecting me from retaliation. It's good for those job applicants who take my advice and get the job. But it only helps those individuals. It only helps me. It doesn't do a thing to change the corrupt culture that forced me underground in the first place.

Here's the other thing. My tactics don't always work. Getting people through that interview door, giving them all the right answers, setting them up with the perfect background—it's all useless if the hiring manager is set on discrimination. Or worse, the collective minds of certain managers or the company scheme dictate a quota only allowing so many of a certain race or gender in the door, like that which was alleged at Friedman's jewelry. On top of that, because I don't differentiate based on race or gender or any other factor, including whether the job candidate is a white male, and because white males dominate the business world and the professional white-collar positions I recruit for, a large percentage of them benefit from my underground coaching and advice far more often than women and minorities. They already have the advantage of being automatic members of the good old boys club. The hurdles they have to overcome—age or being labeled overqualified—are substantially reduced on that basis alone. As a group, they are the least affected by the corrupt system.

I challenged that group of managers at Uniforms and the Restaurant Group and threatened to go to the EEOC at FSfoods because helping the few wasn't enough.

I have, to this point, attempted to offer a glimpse of my experience as it happened, including my ambivalence and the related struggle of understanding the corporate culture and the depth of the evil I encountered, whether it involved just individuals, a group, or the whole of the organization. I attempted to show how I vacillated between feelings of faith and hope that fairness is possible versus feelings of anger and a contempt for what I believed at times was a concerted effort to control, dominate, and crush individual spirit. I hope that with this book I've been able to convey my inner struggle to find reasons to deny the existence of a conspiratorial corporate construct, that finds it beneficial to maintain the cultural divide between races and genders, the strong and the weak.

However, after years of experiencing the same thing over and over again, combined with years of research, I have come to a very clear understanding of the corporate cultural scheme in relation to American society as a whole and Americans as individuals.

Robert Kennedy Jr. points out that, "legally, corporations cannot do good things. They cannot do true philanthropy, they can't do things that are good for our country or our communities. We want corporations to be this way, to focus narrowly. We want them to focus narrowly on shareholder value."

In that vein, they have no interest in ensuring an inclusive workforce. Kennedy also said, "We would be nuts to let them anywhere near our government because we designed them to plunder—and that's what they're going to do to us if we let them run our country. That's what they're doing now. That's why from the beginning of our national history, our greatest political leaders, Republicans and Democrats, have been warning Americans against the domination of corporate power. Teddy Roosevelt, a Republican, said that

America would never be destroyed by a foreign enemy, by an Osama bin Laden. But he also warned that our Bill of Rights, our Constitution, and our treasured democratic institutions would be subverted by malefactors of great wealth who would steal them from within."

Failure to challenge out in the open provides comfort to the enemy, as well as easing the conscience of those who go along, help, and cover for them. It does nothing for the greater task that has been explained through writings of the likes of civil liberties activist and author Tom Head. I have taken some liberties in applying his writing to the American workplace.

Head wrote about the history and affects of institutional racism in our society as a whole. I have applied his writing to my thesis on the workplace, replacing the words institutional racism with institutional discrimination.

The term "institutional discrimination" describes systemic patterns that have the net effect of imposing oppressive or otherwise negative conditions against identifiable groups on the basis of race, age, gender, ethnicity, disability, religion, sexual orientation, and other illegal and legal forms of discrimination, including employment status; aspects of physical appearance, such as weight, height, and relative attractiveness; and personal lifestyle.

Head originally applied those words to racism, noting that the term "institutional racism" was coined by civil rights activist Stokely Carmichael (later known as Kwame Ture) during the late 1960s.

Head wrote: "Carmichael felt that it was necessary to distinguish between personal bias, which has specific effects and can be identified and corrected relatively easily, and institutional bias, which is generally long-term and grounded more in inertia than in intent.

Carmichael made this distinction because, like Martin Luther King Jr., he had grown tired of white moderates and uncommitted liberals who felt that the primary or sole purpose of the civil rights movement was to achieve white personal transformation. Carmichael's primary concern, and the primary concern of most civil rights leaders was and is societal transformation— a much more ambitious goal."

The same can be said for the advancement of the right to equal employment opportunity. Transformation of the individual who commits acts of discrimination in hiring and promotions is essential. However, institutional discrimination, that which is sanctioned by an organization through policies, procedures, or omission of actions against individual perpetrators, is where the transformation is more relevant and essential.

Head wrote: "Institutional racism results from the caste system that sustained, and was sustained by, slavery and racial segregation. Although the laws that enforced this caste system are no longer in place, its basic structure still stands to this day. This structure may gradually fall apart on its own over a period of generations, but activism is necessary to expedite the process and provide for a more equitable society in the interim."

So it is with the American workplace. However, this concept has to broaden to include all forms of discrimination and unfair and unequal treatment. Bias based on gender, age, disability, religion, nationality, sexual orientation, physical appearance, marital status, and being unemployed is just as much a part of the paradigm as racism. Despite the laws on the books, the basic structure still stands, but, unfortunately, there are few signs that the structure will gradually fall apart on its own over time.

For the sake of argument, let us assume that the structure will eventually fall apart. Forget about the new surge in discrimination, the fact that the unemployed are openly discriminated against simply because they are unemployed. Set aside the fact that companies are free to determine the employability of workers based on their risky personal habits and activities outside the workplace, like smoking. Forget about the fact that, for the first time since such records were kept, complaints of retaliation in the workplace to the EEOC have exceeded those of race discrimination. Set aside the fact that women are still paid 25 percent less than men for the same job.

Activism is still needed to expedite the process and provide for a more equitable workplace in the interim because as we wait for the generational change individuals and their families are affected on a daily basis.

Beyond my belief that none of us can shrink from being engaged in the "bigger task," beyond the argument of being motivated to confront evil, I confess that it's also true that I have very little control of my reaction when I am confronted by the evils of discrimination. Even if I wanted to look the other way, even if thoughts of retaliation entered my mind, reflex of conscience spurred by righteous indignation forces me to challenge it.

I am equally compelled by fear. Fear of being one of the drones I have described in this writing. Fear of going to the dark side as Liz did. Fear of betraying my race, like Milton and Kathy betrayed their heritage for a seat at the table; like the minorities who urged Harmeen Jones to keep his head down in the midst of racism at Fox News; like Julie, who expected me to play the game and go along with discrimination at Kprints. Like all the other characters who have yielded their individualism, not knowing or understanding that they were sacrificing their freedom and risking opportunities for their children and their children's children.

I suggest that individuals—whether they are seeking employment or are employed and part of the corporate apparatus that keeps others down—at the very least, need to defy the corrupt process, even if it is for no other reason than to save themselves.

The ultimate goal in providing this unvarnished view of the corporate America I've experienced is to not only awaken individuals to the injustices they face, but also the magnitude of it, how it threatens their lives, and how they are an unwitting party to their own destruction.

Institutional discrimination is part and parcel of the overall threat corporations pose to the United States, and thereby individual freedoms, which we have been warned about by voices far greater than mine.

Thomas Jefferson, FDR, and Abraham Lincoln all warned America about corporations. Jefferson said, "I hope we shall take warning from the example of England and crush in its birth the aristocracy of our moneyed corporations which dare already to challenge our Government to trial, and bid defiance to the laws of our country."

Lincoln said, "The money powers prey upon the nation in times of peace and conspire against it in times of adversity. It is more despotic than a monarchy, more insolent than autocracy, and more selfish than bureaucracy. It denounces as public enemies all who question its methods or throw light upon its crimes... corporations have been enthroned and an era of corruption in high places will follow, and the money powers of the country will endeavor to prolong its reign by working upon the prejudices of the people until all wealth is aggregated in a few hands and the Republic is destroyed."

Franklin Delano Roosevelt warned, "The liberty of a democracy is not safe if the people tolerate the growth of private power to a point where it becomes stronger than their democratic state itself. That, in its essence, is Fascism—ownership of government by an individual, by a group or by any controlling private power."

At the end of his presidency, Dwight Eisenhower gave a farewell address to the nation. In it, he warned Americans of the military-industrial complex: "We must guard against the acquisition of unwarranted influence, whether sought or unsought, by the military-industrial complex. The potential for the disastrous rise of misplaced power exists and will persist. We must never let the weight of this combination endanger our liberties or democratic processes. We should take nothing for granted. Only an alert and knowledgeable citizenry can compel the proper meshing of the huge industrial and military machinery of defense with our peaceful methods and goals, so that security and liberty may prosper together."

Robert Kennedy Jr. referred to the "corrosive impact of excessive corporate power in democracy."

Over the past ten years, journalist, political spokesman, and broadcaster Bill Moyers, plying over fifty years of experiencing and studying the world, has passionately written about how our government works and the role of the individual in society. He has warned of "a political system increasingly at the mercy of a corporate ruling class."

The only true threat to losing our democracy comes through and by the apathy of the citizenry. Collective power, whether it is the military-industrial complex or the corporate-industrial complex, or the power of a single individual, as FDR said, cannot succeed if we don't allow it.

Of all the many tactics the corporate complex has utilized to accomplish the dominance warned of by these great Americans, none has been more insidious than that which was predicted by Lincoln: "It denounces as public enemies all who question its methods or throw light upon its crimes."

It was Margaret Mead, the American anthropologist, who said, "Never doubt that a small group of thoughtful, committed citizens can change the world. Indeed, it is the only thing that ever has."

The corporate attack on individualism comes from knowledge that Margaret Mead's words ring true and, thus, destruction of those of us who would defy, question methods, or throw light upon crimes is essential in order to complete the kind of domination we have been warned of throughout history.

I told you about Ted Maines and FedEx. What I didn't tell you was the comment his attorney made after he won that $1.5 million verdict. Jill Schwartz, who represented Maines, said, "We can never stop discrimination in the workplace if the very people who have the courage to oppose it are silenced."

An EEOC attorney involved in the case described Maines as courageous for speaking out against acts of discrimination.

The comments from plaintiffs victorious in lawsuits always seem to have the same theme: "I knew the truth would prevail." While that may have been the case in their situations, the truth about the system as a whole is still kept hostage. Retaliation continues to maintain the silence of many. And therein lies my final answer to the comments and questions I began this chapter with. Corporate money and power has engulfed our government, electing officials who have seen to it that agencies like the EEOC are limited in their power to represent individuals and manipulating laws to favor the corporate agenda. But all the money in the world cannot bribe every individual. It is only by way of convincing the masses that no evil exists and silencing the voices of those who would alert the world to their scheme that the corporate construct will succeed.

The lead plaintiff in the Texaco case, Bari-Ellen Roberts, stood up against the corporate giant not knowing how she would fare during the process or whether she would win. While others would join her, in the beginning, she stood alone. Ted Maines stood alone, as did Marion Shaub and many of the other people I have used as examples throughout this book. I stood alone at FSfoods, Restaurant Group, and Kprints. But here's the thing. While I stood alone at the Uniforms meeting in February 2010 when I challenged those managers and the company to end discriminatory practices, there were others who were fighting the battle, as well. And like Roberts and others, revelations from my discrimination complaint spurred others to do the same. By the time I left Uniforms, five HR representatives had filed discrimination-related complaints against the company, as well as three operations and sales managers. Others came forward internally. And although those individuals were forced out and saw little to no relief for their efforts, and many others simply walked away from that corrupt culture, a growing number are standing up to the unfairness they face and that which is inflicted upon others.

Every individual who stands, either by himself or herself or as part of a group, provides the inspiration and courage for others to do the same. With each new person challenging the inherently corrupt system—whether it is through heeding my advice to go by their own rules to get a job, protecting themselves as an employee, or standing against crimes they witness as opposed to being party to them—individualism grows and festers as a thorn in the side of the corporate-industrial complex. It picks at corporate strategy to maintain the structure of pitting the haves against the have-nots and the strong over the weak, generally defined as whites against minorities, men against women.

Through that growth, we, at the very least, stay the corporate agenda to quash our individualism. Eventually individuals evolve into that small group of people Mead spoke of. Eventually, the masses (Occupy Wall Street) heed the dire warnings of the likes of Jefferson and Lincoln and call upon their elective representatives to take action to restore the collective voice of the citizenry. In mass, we insist on reaffirmation of the safeguards that protect individual freedom and the constitutional right to fair and equal treatment in all aspects of our lives—not the least of which is the right to work.

Some argue that we have already lost the battle. They echo what Kalle Lasn, filmmaker, author, magazine editor, and activist, wrote: "We, the people, have lost control. Corporations, these legal fictions that we ourselves created two centuries ago, now have more rights, freedoms, and powers than we do. And we accept this as the normal state of affairs. We go to corporations on our knees. *Please* do the right thing, we plead…We've spent so much time bowed down in deference, we've forgotten how to stand up straight." He argues, "The unofficial history of America, which continues to be written, is not a story of rugged individualism and heroic personal sacrifice in the pursuit of a dream. It is a story of democracy derailed, of a revolutionary spirit suppressed, and of a once-proud people reduced to servitude."

Although it is a substantial argument to demonstrate that that's where we may be headed, in the battle for equal employment opportunity, the Bari-Ellen Robertses of the world have proven that his view is not true—yet.

And therein is the reason I will never stop in my endeavor to bring this issue to the forefront. Hope is renewed every time another person challenges the status quo. I plan to be a part of that, encouraging and advising individuals to defy the inherently corrupt and discriminatory culture until there is a realization that we are not just individuals, but we are collectively the people with rights to equal and fair treatment.

About the Author

Brian Nord is a former corporate recruiting executive turned employee rights advocate and author. In 2011 he founded NFI Associates (www.nfiassociates.com) a business that provides career counseling to job seekers as well as recruiting, staffing, and diversity advancement training and development consulting to corporations.

He has more than twenty years experience on the front lines. His clients include employees, managers, and executives from large and small companies.

Nord is a regular contributor to blogs and on-line newspapers, and has several non-fiction and fiction books in the works.

To reach Nord: send email inquiry to nord@nfiassociates.net

www.ingramcontent.com/pod-product-compliance
Lightning Source LLC
Chambersburg PA
CBHW020735180526
45163CB00001B/246